TVR

JOHN TIPLER

SUTTON PUBLISHING LIMITED

Sutton Publishing Limited
Phoenix Mill · Stroud
Gloucestershire · GL5 2BU

First published in 1998

Reprinted in 2000

Copyright © John Tipler, 1998

British Library Cataloguing in Publication Data
A catalogue record for this book is available from the
British Library

ISBN 0 7509 1766 0

Typeset in 10/12pt Perpetua
Typesetting and origination by
Sutton Publishing Limited.
Printed in Great Britain by
Ebenezer Baylis, Worcester.

Success in motor racing leads to fresh orders, and this was what spurred TVR's ambitious directors Brian Hopton and
Keith Aitchison to implement TVR's legendary attempt at a class win in the Le Mans 24 Hours in 1962. They hired ex-
Standard-Triumph competitions manager Ken Richardson to mastermind the project, and within two months three Mark
IIAs were ready for the Sebring 12-Hour race in Florida. They were powered by 1622cc MGA units, equipped with HRG
heads, high-lift cam, MGA twin-cam con-rods and twin 45DCOE Weber carbs, and developed 125bhp. Two cars retired,
while the Mark Donohue/Gerry Sagerman car was running behind the leading Porsches at one stage. With David Hives
in charge of race preparation three fresh cars were readied for the Le Mans epic. They were painted white with dark
green stripes, and the bonnets were pierced with Ferrari GTO-style cooling ducts to counteract severe overheating
problems. Sadly these were inadequate, and only the Peter Bolton/Ninian Sanderson car started, retiring on the third lap
with a blown head gasket. Here is Ninian Sanderson in one of the works cars at Brands Hatch in August 1962.

CONTENTS

TVRs were driven in competition almost from the word go, and were usually competitive if not always reliable. This is B. Battin's Grantura Mark II approaching Druids Hill bend in a sprint meeting at Brands Hatch (pre-Armco) on 8 April 1962. Home-made race numbers reveal it to be primarily a road car, while headlights are taped over to stop glass falling on to the track in the event of a breakage. Racing-style wing mirrors are fitted, as are extra straps to prevent the bonnet coming adrift. Other contemporary TVR racers included David 'Bunty' Scott Moncrieff and his wife Averil, John Thurner, Arnold Burton, Keith Aitchison, Colin Escott, Anthony Oakes-Richards, Chris Summers, Ninian Sanderson and Tommy Entwistle.

INTRODUCTION

TVR's origins sprang from the humble innovations of a young Blackpool-based engineer, Trevor Wilkinson, in 1947. He built himself a succession of specials in the early 1950s, and to create an identity for these glorified cigar tubes he extracted three letters from his Christian name and TVR was born. Success in minor local competitions created an enthusiastic following, and spawned orders for similar cars. Trevor could either supply complete kits or fully built cars to the customers' own specification. To ensure that they would be reliable he used BMC engines and transmissions, sourced from the local dealers.

The fibreglass industry was booming in the mid-'50s, and a number of sports car bodyshells were available. DIY builders usually applied them to Ford Popular chassis, although Wilkinson's tubular steel chassis were more sophisticated than most. In 1953 he clad them with RGS Atalanta shells, then went on to adapt a pair of front sections from a Microplas Mistral body, one at the front and one at the back, with a simple centre section incorporating a roof, doors and sills. He took a mould from it and went into fibreglass production himself.

By 1955 Trevor had a customer in the USA called Ray Saidel, whom he supplied with rolling chassis. Saidel clothed them in sports racing bodyshells, and under the Jomar name they enjoyed a measure of competition success. Inspired by Saidel's recommendations, a coupé-bodied TVR was shown at the New York Auto Show in 1957, and such was its enthusiastic reception that TVR's first production car, the Grantura, was launched a year later.

However, Trevor got into financial difficulties in 1958, and in what was to be the most unsettled period in its history, TVR liquidated to become Layton Sports Cars – so-called as the factory was located in the Layton suburb of Blackpool at the time. Alongside this operation Grantura Engineering Ltd was set up to procure components, while Layton Sports Cars built the bodies and assembled the cars. Trevor was now joined by several enthusiast-businessmen, and the new managing director Henry Moulds set about increasing production, even though this was contrary to Trevor's policy of methodical development. Next man in the driving seat was Arnold Burton, a scion of the tailoring family and a devoted TVR enthusiast, and with a new investor at the helm fortunes improved for a short while.

As Trevor Wilkinson retreated into the background of the production process, two ambitious local garage proprietors, Brian Hopton and Keith Aitchison, gained control of the company in 1961. The chassis was redesigned by John Thurner, the new technical director, lured from Rolls-Royce in 1959, and the significantly improved result was the Mark II Grantura of 1961, available with Coventry Climax or MGA 1600 engines.

The new regime began competition activity in earnest. They set their sights on Le Mans, and with ex-Triumph competitions manager Ken Richardson in charge, things ought to have gone better. Three works-prepared Mark IIA Granturas competed in the 1962 Sebring 12-Hours, and another three took part in the 1962 Tulip Rally, leading their class for a while. Expectations of early success were to end in debacle, as at Le Mans all three cars were beset with overheating problems. Only one started and retired after three laps, and it was a similar story in the RAC Tourist Trophy.

Meanwhile Trevor Wilkinson had left to form his own fibreglass company, but in 1963 a significant new model was introduced – the TVR Griffith – which was fundamentally a Grantura with a modified chassis and a big American V8 under the bonnet. Then in 1965, with the failure of the stylish new Trident model, another financial crisis obliged Arnold Burton to close the company down.

TVR's salvation appeared in November 1965 in the shape of 23-year old Martin Lilley and his father Arthur, and they began to consolidate the firm at its Hoo Hill factory. Over the next few years the company gradually prospered, with the Grantura being replaced by the Vixen and the Griffith by the Tuscan V8. The 2500 model was introduced specifically for the emissions-sensitive US market, powered by the 2.5-litre straight-six Triumph engine.

Then late in 1970 the company relocated to its current site in Bristol Avenue, where the premises have been expanded enormously over the last twenty years. The new factory brought with it a major development in styling, chassis and drivetrain specifications. Using ideas developed in the wide-bodied Tuscan hybrid of 1970, the M-series cars were introduced in 1971. Power-units available in the M-series chassis included the 3.0-litre Ford Essex V6, Triumph 2.5-litre straight six, Ford Kent 1600cc unit, and Triumph 1300cc in very small numbers. The M-series served TVR extremely well through the 1970s, and by 1976 the Taimar hatchback version was available in naturally aspirated and turbocharged form. The following year the convertible 3000S came out – a production first for TVR – and this too was available as a turbo version.

The 1970s had been a period of growth and relative stability at TVR, but it was about to undergo a sea change. Martin Lilley decided a radical shift of styling was in order, and in 1980 the Tasmin was introduced with a new chassis, a new wedge-shaped body and a new engine. Power came from the Ford 2.8-litre V6 Ford Cologne unit, and there were coupé, convertible and 2+2 models. Unfortunately the Tasmin was perceived as being too expensive, rather dated in design, and launched just as a recession gained momentum. With the supply of cars to the USA in disarray through no fault of his own, Lilley had no option but to withdraw, handing over in 1982 to Peter Wheeler who by this time was a major shareholder.

The following year the first of the Rover V8-engined TVRs was introduced, the 350i, and in quick succession the wedge-shaped monsters became faster and more sophisticated, culminating in the mighty 450SEAC of 1988, which produced 324bhp from its 4.5-litre V8 engine.

The S-range ushered in a new chapter in TVR's history in 1987. Although it looked superficially like the old M-series, the S was an entirely new car, priced to attract a fresh generation of TVR buyers. Wheeler's foresight paid off, and it transformed TVR's fortunes to the extent that production almost doubled in a year. However, it was the sleek, all-new Griffith that was really responsible for TVR's renaissance. This model was overwhelmingly successful, and the first cars were delivered to customers at the beginning of 1992. The larger-capacity Griffith 500 came out in 1993, along with the hunkier-looking TVR Chimaera and the longer 2+2-bodied Cerbera, and they consolidated TVR's current position as the most prolific of Britain's independent car manufacturers.

The TVR Tuscan Challenge started in 1989, and became the world's fastest one-marque race series. With 450bhp from a car weighing only 800kg, the Tuscans were spectacularly fast and developed a reputation for providing huge dramas in the corners. It wasn't long before a Cerbera was competing in the FIA Global GT Challenge, and the mighty 240mph Speed Twelve prototype, launched in 1997, was set to make an assault on the Le Mans 24 Hours.

CHAPTER ONE

TREVOR'S TRIALS AND TRIBULATIONS

Trevor Wilkinson began building specials as a hobby in a workshop in Blackpool in 1947. He made chassis to order, and by 1955 he was exporting a handful of cars to the USA. As TVR's identity began to take shape, there followed a succession of financial collapses, name changes and take-overs that saw its founder retire in 1963. In 1997 he was elected President of the TVR Car Club.

Bordering on the 'art deco' style, this was the TVR logo up to and including the Grantura Mark IIA. By 1962 – coinciding with the rise and fall of TVR Cars Limited, the emergence of Grantura Engineering and implementation of the new Thurner-designed chassis – most cars carried the new simpler badge that just said TVR with no fancy frills.

This is TVR 2, the second vehicle to be built by the marque's founder Trevor Wilkinson, in 1949. It took pride of place on the TVR Car Club stand at the 1997 International Classic Car Show, having been restored by owner Richard Wright. It is the earliest surviving TVR, as its predecessor – notionally TVR 1 – was written off in a racing accident, and its successor, TVR 3, was scrapped. All three had identical spaceframe chassis, clad in aluminium cigar-tube bodies broadly similar to this, and the specification consisted of a motley assortment of components dating back to 1910. It is powered by an 1172cc side-valve Ford engine, the suspension is ex-Austin Devon and the back axle from a Morris 8, and the rev-counter is from a Spitfire fighter plane.

A 1955 TVR rolling chassis, 7C101, fitted with a 1098cc overhead camshaft Coventry Climax FWA engine, mated to an MGA gearbox, and using VW trailing arm suspension and steering. It was part of a small consignment supplied to one of Trevor Wilkinson's first customers, US foreign car specialist Ray Saidel. His import business was based near Boston at Merrimack Street Garage, Manchester, New Hampshire, and with engineers Norman Leeds and Louie Turner he clad them with his own aluminium sports-racing bodies, and named them Jomars. The name was an amalgamation of his daughter's names, Joanna and Mary Lou. Seven of the original twenty-four Jomar-TVRs survive.

The Jomar story is significant to TVR's early history, because by racing the TVR chassis its deficiencies came to be ironed out. Ray Saidel was also responsible for suggesting the coupé styling that would endure for twenty-five years. His Merrimack Street garage was an Oldsmobile dealership as well as having franchises for Alfa Romeo, Triumph, MG, Porsche and Mercedes Benz, and Saidel's career with sports cars took off with an Oldsmobile V8-powered Allard J2 and a pair of rugged Dellow trials car chassis in 1955. These were clad in aluminium to create the Mark 1 Jomar. The Dellow chassis was too heavy, so he ordered one from TVR, and in June 1956 he took delivery of TVR chassis 7C101, one of the first to be made at the Hoo Hill factory. Racing his aluminium-bodied Jomar 7C101 in SCCA events at circuits like Watkins Glen, Lime Rock and Bridgehampton, kingpin failures were numerous. The factory responded by curing this and other defects, and Saidel went ahead with another two more powerful Climax-engined Jomar-TVR sports racers. By 1957 all three Jomars were racing and finishing well. A pair of similarly styled cars in fibreglass was made in the UK (see Andrew Houston's car, page 11) and one was exported to Ray Saidel. He was appointed TVR's US distributor in 1956, although in reality cars were dispatched only in ones and twos. The roadster body was much admired, but neither Saidel nor his many aspiring dealers were much impressed by the three right-hand drive notch-back coupés dispatched to him, and he suggested TVR produce a fastback body, which of course they did. At the 1958 New York Motor Show there was more interest in Jomar-TVRs than the factory could possibly cope with. The coupé was badged and sold as the Jomar in the US and the TVR Grantura in the UK, and the car illustrated here belongs to Al Way from New Jersey. It is chassis 7/C/114, and has done just 6,700 miles from new. TVR Jomars could be specified either with 85bhp 1098cc Climax or 61bhp Shorrock-supercharged 1172cc Ford engines, and this one has the Climax unit.

According to Ray's son Alex, the product was much improved by the end of 1958, and Ray took many class wins with Jomar-TVRs that year. He even raced Jomar 7C113 with a blown 1200 Climax engine at the USAC 1,000-mile road race at Daytona in 1959. Chassis 7C111A was converted into an open-wheel Formula 2 car that year, and campaigned into the 1960s with Oldsmobile V8 power. At a meeting at Blackpool in 1959 Saidel was invited to take just six cars in 1960, and twenty-five cars a year after that, which seemed feasible. However, TVR's management – Layton Sports Cars – subsequently insisted he take fifty cars straight away, which he declined to do and, somewhat disenchanted, Ray gave up on TVR altogether.

Trevor Wilkinson and Jack Pickard created the first multi-tubular TVR chassis in 1949, and this one with its Ford 100E steering wheel is the 1955 prototype chassis 7C101 destined for Ray Saidel in the States. Kit cars were a recognised way of building one's own vehicle in the make-do era of British post-war austerity, and significantly there was an additional advantage in that cars built from kits were exempt from purchase tax. So while customers bought rolling chassis from TVR Engineering and fitted their own bodyshells, the company itself only made a handful of finished cars. In the 1950s enthusiast constructors could choose from a wide selection of fibreglass styles, most of which were loosely modelled on successful sports racing cars of the period. In 1960 a TVR Grantura cost £880 in kit form, with the MGA engine as standard, but rather less with Ford 105E and more for Coventry Climax power.

The TVR coupé body shape was evolved from a pair of Microplas Mistral nose cones, one facing forwards and the other for the rear, joined by a rounded roof section, doors, sills and undertray. The rear of this notch-back coupé, pictured in 1957, shows how the shape was resolved. In what had originally been designed as a nose cone, the headlight housings were completely filled in, the engine bay became the boot space, and the radiator aperture was blanked off. It now provided a location for the rear lights and numberplate, while the spare wheel was mounted on the bootlid. This car measured 11ft 6in long with a 7ft wheelbase, 4ft 4in track front and rear, and was powered by a 1098cc Coventry Climax engine coupled to an MG gearbox. Of the six notch-back coupés made, one had an MG 1500cc engine, and one was modified to become the definitive TVR coupé prototype.

The trailing arm independent rear suspension on the 1957 TVR chassis was derived for the most part from the front end of the Volkswagen Beetle. The cast alloy suspension uprights were specially made, as were the transmission housing and drive shafts. This suspension set-up was used between 1956 and 1962, which included Grantura coupé Marks I, II and III, as well as the Jomar sports racers.

This TVR roadster was discovered lying derelict in a Perthshire farmyard by Andrew Houston, who eventually bought the remains in the late 1970s and restored it over a number of years. There was initially some confusion as to its provenance: it looked like a Jomar-TVR, but it had a fibreglass body, so was it a Jomar or a TVR? This was clarified by Ray Saidel, who identified it as a TVR roadster made at Blackpool in 1957. Certain key features enabled him to identify it, including its exposed Morris Minor door hinges (others were hidden), its full-race five-bearing Coventry Climax 1100cc engine that had a bigger oil gallery welded into the block, and perhaps most significantly, a Morris Minor gearbox that had been donated by Jack Pickard. Trevor Wilkinson was less keen on producing roadsters than GT cars, which accounted for the direction the company took.

When Andrew Houston began restoring this TVR roadster he found its fibreglass body was relatively primitive, since it was originally made with no gel-coat and was thus rather uneven. It is one of a pair of sports-racing cars built on the 7C chassis by Trevor Wilkinson, and its sister was shipped to Ray Saidel, contemporary with the first alloy-bodied Jomars. Seen in profile, its origins in the pair of Microplas Mistral nose cones is clear. Andrew Houston raced the car quite extensively and with some success in historic events in the UK until 1993.

TVRs never had opening boots, until the Taimar hatchback model of 1976. However this 1962 Mark III Grantura does, and the semi-circular bulge below the rear valance indicates that its spare wheel is accommodated in the boot. The car belongs to Ernest Blakeman, who got the idea of 'putting the boot in' when he got a puncture one rainy night back in the early 1970s.

In 1956 Trevor Wilkinson took out a lease on a disused brickworks on the Hoo Hill industrial estate on Bisphen Road in the Blackpool suburb of Layton. Much of the proceeds from the sale of the previous Beverley Grove works were used to refurbish the new factory. Foreman Jack Pickard reorganised the premises as a car plant, with chassis welding in the old brick kilns, body manufacture on the first floor, and final assembly in a separate building. Pictured with a new Grantura Mark I are Wilkinson, centre, Pickard, left, and machine shop manager John Ward. Note the lack of embellishments on the front wings, minimal metal bumpers and absence of quarter-lights. By this time TVR sales manager was former motorcycle speedway star Bernard Williams, with Bolton businessman and engineer Fred Thomas as financial backer. It was a period of constant transition, and by 1960 Arnold Burton of the Leeds-based tailoring family fulfilled this role.

By January 1958 the Grantura shape had been resolved to incorporate the unusually large, curved rear windscreen, redolent of the Jensen 541 and contemporary Chevrolet Corvette coupé, and the TVR fuel filler was now located on the right hand side. The lines of the Grantura roof were the inspiration of Ray Saidel, whose potential customers found the original TVR notch-back coupé shape 'too ugly', so he recommended the fastback look. The interior of the later Mark I Grantura was quite civilised for its day, with wind-up windows and opening quarter-lights.

The Grantura was available with a choice of power units. This is a 1959 Mark I, made from 1958 to 1960. It was fitted with the 1489cc MGA engine as standard, while the 1098cc or 1216cc Coventry Climax FWE unit was specified by competition drivers. The Mark II ran with the newer 1588cc MGA engine, and could also be fitted with the 997cc 105E Ford Anglia engine or the 1340cc Ford Classic motor, which was significantly better. These replaced the earlier 1172cc Ford 100E sidevalve unit, which was readily tuneable and occasionally fitted with a supercharger. MG gearboxes were normally used, but ZF close ratio boxes could be specified. By 1962 more Granturas were running with 998cc Ford engines than MGA units, although Abingdon's new 1622cc engine had just become available. Grantura transmission was by the four-speed BMC manual gearbox.

Stylistic hallmarks of the Grantura were the big, front-hinged bonnet, the radically curved panoramic rear window and the Ford Consul windscreen that served the company until 1979. As the body evolved with the passage of time, the side windows of the Mark II no longer had opening quarter lights, and the flared lips over the Mark I's front wheelarches were applied to the rear wheelarches of the Mark II. The spare wheel was tucked away behind the 8.75-gallon (40-litre) fuel tank, situated behind the rear axle. This Mark I Grantura pictured in the Yorkshire Dales is chassis number 148, and until 1997 it belonged to Keith Bird. Its correct registration number was 23 JWL, but the car has since been exported. The strangely angled bumper overriders were a TVR optional extra, back in 1959. Grantura specifications were gradually improved, and by 1960 Girling discs replaced the drums at the front, and Alfin drums took the place of 10-in Girling drums at the rear. Dunlop centre-lock wire-spoke wheels shod with 5.5in x 15 Dunlop Gold Seal tyres were standard issue. Those wanting a bit extra out of their cars fitted lightweight aluminium HRG cross-flow cylinder heads to Ford and BMC engines, and Weber carbs often replaced standard SUs. If the car was purchased in kit form, it was assembled at the factory up to the point where the customer had to drop in the engine and radiator. He had also to couple up the drive shaft and half-shafts, fit the front suspension, and connect up the lights and instruments to the wiring loom that had already been fitted. Production volumes were never large in the early days, with just 100 Mark I Granturas like this one made between 1958 and 1960. Four hundred units of the Mark II and IIA were produced between 1960 and 1962, and 90 examples of the MGB-engined Mark III, which was made until 1964. The MGB-powered 1800S and Mark IV 1800S with the so-called Manx-tail body and distinctive Ford Cortina rear lights was produced between 1964 and 1968.

The date is 12 August 1961, and the competition is close at Silverstone in the Birkett Six Hour relay race, as J.B.M. Wadsworth holds off an indecently quick Austin A40 and a Lotus 15 with his Mark II Grantura. This event saw teams competing with machinery as varied as Saabs and D-type Jaguars, and was won in this instance by John Sprinzel's Team Sebring Sprites, followed by the big Healeys and the tyre-smoking Mini team. Normally the TVR's rivals in competition at this time would include other small volume specials like the Marcos, Ginetta, GSM Delta, Diva, Turner, Elva Courier, Warwick, Rochdale Olympic, and of course the Lotus Elite. In this event the TVR team ran out of luck when one of its number ran out of fuel. This Mark I Grantura has an air scoop on the bonnet, and features the extra pair of air intakes above the nose and in the sides of the front wings that distinguished later cars.

This pristine 1963 Grantura Mark IIA belongs to Roger Cook, Cotswolds regional organiser of the TVR Car Club. Note the indicators mounted on the bonnet and sidelights located in the headlight nacelles. When this car was built the factory was operating as TVR Cars once more, rather than Layton Sports Cars, and producing Granturas at the rate of twenty cars a month. By now they were installing sound-deadening material from Pressed Felt to counteract the resonance caused by the naked glass-fibre shell. The Mark III Grantura prototype with its John Thurner-designed chassis was introduced at the New York Salon in 1962, about the same time that a disillusioned Trevor Wilkinson quit the company that he had founded.

You would expect a TVR specialist to run a special TVR, and this superb-looking Mark III Grantura belongs to Steve Reid, who runs Cheshire-based TVR Classics (telephone 01928 719267). He deals particularly in vehicles of this era, although he is not averse to trading the odd TVR wedge model. Steve Reid's Grantura was built in May 1962 when the firm was trading under the Layton Sports Cars banner, and was one of the first with the new John Thurner-designed chassis and contemporary with the ill-starred Le Mans cars. It runs Triumph TR4 brakes, with assistance from a servo normally fitted on the Griffith 200 models. The steering feels light yet precise, owing to its Triumph rack and pinion steering, allied to double wishbone (the lower one is Herald-derived) front suspension. This car has wider rim wire wheels than standard – and chromed in this case – shod with 185/70 x 15 BF Goodrich Comp TA tyres.

Steve Reid bought his Mark III Grantura in bits in 1987 and set about rebuilding it, refurbishing the interior in its austere early-'60s format. He was also able to incorporate an original Grantura steering wheel with its black Bakelite rim, steel spokes and semi-circular horn rim, and trafficator switch. It also has a 1950s TVR logo in the central boss. The aluminium gear-knob on top of a gearchange turret from a Sherpa van made a neater job of the installation. Steve Reid's Mark III left the factory in 1962, powered by a 1622cc MGA engine with an HRG aluminium cross-flow cylinder head and a pair of twin-choke sidedraught Weber carbs. But in the course of its restoration Steve fitted the HRG head and ancillaries to a 1798cc MGB block, mated to an MGB overdrive gearbox. Maximum power is 98bhp at 5400rpm, and maximum torque is 110lb/ft at 3000rpm. It is good for 114mph, being lighter than an MGB GT, and can do the 0–60mph sprint in 9.9 seconds.

Peter Simpson cuts inside an MGB at a Northampton Car Club event at Silverstone in 1964. The Mark III Grantura has evidently undergone a serious bit of surgery on its nose to counter the omnipresent overheating problem, and it is running Lotus 'wobbly-web' alloy wheels.

One consequence of the new Thurner-designed Mark III chassis with its 10-in longer wheelbase was that it was strong enough to take a cast-iron American V8 motor. Inspired by the exploits of the future CanAm and F1 star Mark Donohue in an AC Cobra, the mechanics at US dealer Jack Griffith's garage performed a similar engine swap on Gerry Sagerman's previously MG-powered TVR. Sporting a 289 cu-in Ford V8 motor, the Grantura was tested by Donohue and Gerry Sagerman (who would become TVR's North American concessionaire), and pronounced just about viable. In deference to Jack Griffith, who was confidently expected to sell a lot of TVRs in the States, the V8-engined Grantura was named after him. This 1967 Griffith belongs to John Catt and is pictured thundering down Deer's Leap at Oulton Park in 1993.

Now owned by Don Ensley, this modified Mark III Grantura was Gerry Sagerman's race car, acquired in 1963 after he had tested the Sebring works racer. The engine was blueprinted, ran an IIRG alloy head and 40DCOE Webers, with Koni dampers and 72-spoke wire wheels. It carried Gerry to the SCCA Area 1 Championship title three years running, as well as taking a class win in the 1965 CanAm round at Bridgehampton.

Sagerman was originally asked to represent TVR in the States by Arnold Burton, but only became actively involved in 1965 when the Lilleys took over. Jack Griffith subsequently worked for him as south-east TVR distributor, and the two remain good friends. According to Sagerman, the major frustrations of selling TVRs in the States were dealing with US safety and exhaust controls and sourcing components that complied with them. However, he says his fond rapport with the Lilley family over their twenty-year association made it all worthwhile.

Back in Blackpool in 1963, the Griffith's suspension was strengthened, spring rates and damper settings recalibrated, and the footwells modified to gain space in the engine bay. There was a different exhaust system, naturally, and the bonnet sprouted a bulge to clear the pancake air filter. The car gained wider 5in wire wheel rims shod with 185-section tyres, but the drivetrain remained otherwise unaltered. Despite being regarded as a handful to drive in its day, the classic Griffith has enjoyed a huge renaissance in historic racing, as demonstrated here by Colin Bates at Oulton Park in 1993.

Successful or highly individual racing cars quickly gained an identity for themselves, and the Mongoose of David Plumstead was one such example. It was based on a 1965 Griffith, and ran a standard 4.7-litre Ford V8 engine, but the bodywork was modified to accommodate 8.25in wide-rim Borrani wire wheels and Dunlop R7 race tyres. Here, the Mongoose is not after a Cobra but Peter Lumsden's equally well-known lightweight Jaguar E-Type, going round the outside at Brands Hatch's Druids Hairpin. The event is the BRSCC GT Sports Car race, 18 July 1965 – note spectators up the tree – with Bernard Unett's Sunbeam Tiger and a Diva GT in hot pursuit. The Jaguar beat the Mongoose on this occasion. The Mongoose subsequently had its nose radically altered, and became known as the Vandervell GT (opposite, top) at Castle Combe, when it was campaigned in the 1967 *Motoring News* Special GT Championship by Mike Greenwood for Clive Vandervell and Martin Colvill's Purley Performance Cars team. Thirty years on it was restored to its original 1965 specification and blue and white livery and (opposite, bottom) prepared to full FIA Appendix K regulations by Phil Stott Performance Engineering for owner Stephen Smith to participate in HSCC prodsports events.

The 4.7-litre Ford V8-engined TVR became identified as the Griffith, after the man whose mechanics supposedly conceived it, and in some respects it set the standard for TVR products of the future: a lightweight, competition-derived chassis and bodyshell, propelled by a massive power unit. Jack Griffith was permitted to market the car separately from TVR's official agent Dick Monnich, and he showed the prototype at the 1963 Boston Motor Show. A 195bhp model known as the Griffith 200 gave way in 1964 to the more powerful 271bhp Griffith 400 with three-barrel downdraught Holley carburettor, which had a bigger radiator and Kenlowe electric fan. This is Joe Ward's Cambridge Motorsport-prepared Griffith in the paddock at Silverstone for a round of the Pre-1965 Historic Sportscars championship. Note the elaborate cross bracing of the roll cage and the competition filler cap.

The Griffith 400 was based on the Mark III Grantura body/chassis and its aerodynamically improved Kamm- or Manx-tail featured the Cortina Mk 1 rear lights, often referred to as 'ban-the-bomb' lights because they resemble an inverted CND logo. The bonnet bulge that accommodates the air filter over the 4.7-litre Ford V8 engine is prominent.

Like the Grantura Mark III on which it was based, Griffith suspension was sourced from Triumph, and included Vitesse coil springs and Herald lower wishbones, together with TVR's own tubular wishbone for the upper link, front anti-roll bar and telescopic dampers all round. There was a second set of dampers at the rear. Steering was Triumph rack and pinion, with 10.75in Girling discs all round. It was a phenomenal performer in its day, and with a 0–60mph time of 5 seconds and a top speed of 160mph, it could outpace most contemporary thoroughbred sportscars. This car is a 1967 model, belonging to Simon Bridge, who currently uses it in sprints and hillclimbs. It is chassis number 200/010, and was the last Griffith to be built out of a batch of ten after Martin Lilley took over at TVR. Only four of these were in right-hand drive.

There's no substitute for cubic capacity, as demonstrated by the Griffith of Roger Arveschoug, who has just out-braked the MGA for the corner at Silverstone. There is little wonder really, as the TVR has a particularly rare specification. It has a 5.0-litre Ford V8 engine and close-ratio gearbox, reputedly prepared originally by Holman and Moody, who ran some of the works' Ford GT40s in the mid-'60s along with Shelby American Inc. But in this instance the engine may have been built for a Daytona Cobra to race at Le Mans. It consists of a four-bolt block with big-valve heads, Indy rods, pop-up pistons and Coopers rings, a baffled sump and Le Mans-modified oil system, Sullivan race cams, and four 48IDA Weber carburettors with shortened intake trumpets.

One of the most successful Griffith 400s to race in historic events is the DG Motorsport International prepared 1965 car of Kerry Horan, pictured in one of the rounds of the 1993 FIA European GT cup for Historic Sports Cars, in which he won Class A outright. It has raced at several European circuits, including Monza, Zolder, the Salzburgring, Knutsdorp and Montlhéry, where Horan held his own against the cream of European historic sports machinery including E-types, Mustangs, Corvettes and Ferraris. The car is Griffith 400 chassis 'number two' and was discovered in the USA and restored by Chris Schirle and Julian Knapp at DG Motorsport on a brand new chassis. It is powered by a genuine Hi-Po 289 cu-in Ford V8 also sourced in the States. An F1-type swirl-pot fed by a bleed pipe from the radiator helps ensure it suffers none of the traditional overheating problems.

The Grantura 1800S was powered by the MGB engine and 133 were made in the two years between 1964 and 1966. This is a 1965 example, built at the time when Grantura Engineering was foundering in the midst of financial crises. These centred on the US recession and a dock strike that paralysed the Griffith operation, plus wrangling over the naming of the Trident prototype, and management incompatibility that combined to drive an exasperated Arnold Burton to close up the TVR factory gates.

CHAPTER TWO

BOOM TIME AT TVR

It was the whirlwind mid-'60s, when anything was possible and people tried everything. Twenty-three-year-old Martin Lilley and his father Arthur bought the remains of the mis-managed Grantura Engineering, and set about establishing TVR Engineering as a successful specialist sports car manufacturer.

A motley collection of BMC, Triumph and Ford products, but not a TVR in sight at the Hoo Hill plant in 1966. Meanwhile, a pensive Arthur Lilley contemplates the future.

This immaculate Mark IV 1800S Grantura pictured in a quintessentially Dutch landscape belongs to Netherlands TVR Car Club member Dick de Bruyn of Wijdenes, Holland. It is chassis number 18/093, works order 67/0118, and signed off at the factory on 25 April 1967. One of only seventy-eight units made, this car has the wooden dash that slopes down to the transmission tunnel. Unusually, it was finished with a Vixen bonnet, which is an oversight typical in a time of transition. This was the last model to have the rounded top to the side windows; with the later Vixen and Tuscan models it became more sharply pointed. Martin Lilley and his father had taken over at TVR Engineering in November 1965, and still relied on Bernard Williams, Tommy Entwistle and John Ward at the now independent Grantura Plastics to produce the bodyshells. While differential casings, hub carriers and wishbones were made in-house, suspension consisted of a combination of Triumph Herald, Spitfire and Standard 8 components. Cars were trimmed at the Hoo Hill factory after painting at the Nissen huts on Marton Moss, and sold in kit form on the home market, and exported as fully built cars.

One reason for bringing out the Vixen in October 1967 was to launch the new Ford engine and, by introducing a new name, to distance the company from its earlier reputation for irregular build quality. The Vixen S1 used the Grantura Mark IV chassis and Manx-tail bodywork, which included the Mark 1 Cortina rear light clusters (taped over in this case) and door handles that incorporated the locks. Only the badge on the rear panel and a single broad air intake on the bonnet identified this model from the Mark IV 1800S. Twelve Vixen S1s were fitted with the outgoing MGB engine, while the remaining 105 got the Ford 1600GT motor. This 1967 Vixen S1 is in the Donington Park paddock for the TVR Car Club's Extravaganza meeting.

Viewed from straight ahead, the bonnet air scoop on this 1967 Vixen S1 is clearly evident, and the raised moulding continues up to merge with the rear of the bonnet. While the bonnet air intake and vent arrangements of the subsequent S2 and Tuscan model are peculiar to TVR, the S1's air intake has the look of Aston Martin or Ferrari exotica about it. Other features here include indicators at either side of the mesh radiator grille and tiny side indicators in the wings beside the headlights.

While the dashboard of the Vixen S1 is comprehensively equipped with dials and switchgear, and a fire extinguisher in this case, it all gives the impression of being rather chaotic, perhaps exaggerated by the wrinkled leather covering of the transmission tunnel. The chassis had yet to be lengthened, so the S1 still had relatively small door openings.

The notion of a rear-engined TVR had been around since 1962, and TVR's race preparation specialist David Hives advocated using an Austin 1800 platform and powertrain as the basis. With his sights set on the Fiat 850 Spider and Coupé, designer Trevor Fiore favoured the smaller 850cc Hillman Imp running gear, however. He created a couple of prototypes in steel, and the resulting Tina was displayed at the Turin Show in 1966. The Tina was conceived at a time of major changes at TVR and was therefore possibly always doomed to fail. Although the prototype roadster and coupé were built in steel, the Lilleys' intention was to make the production cars in glass-fibre, subject to finding the necessary funding and making space available in the Hoo Hill factory. The convertible version was shown at the Turin Motor Show in 1966 and again in 1967 with revised frontal treatment. The Tina's highly tuneable rear-mounted Hillman Imp Sport engine promised much, and like the junior exotic Fiat 850 models that it was intended to compete with, the lack of weight under the bonnet was manifest in the front wheels' slightly absurd positive camber. At the Earls Court Show in 1967 the TVR stand was besieged by punters keen to order the Tina. But since the factory was incapable of responding to this unprecedented demand, Martin Lilley approached other manufacturers like Jensen and Aston Martin to explore the possibility of having them make the Tina under licence. They were either too committed in other directions or too reserved, and Lilley forfeited the £15,000 he had personally invested in the project's development costs.

In 1962 one of the owners of TVR Cars Ltd, Brian Hopton, proposed to clothe a Mark III chassis in a stylish Italianate body, and commissioned Frank Costin to draw one. Nothing came of this, but Trevor Fiore, a Paris-based English draughtsman (whose real name was Trevor Frost) who had genuine family connections with the Turin styling house Fissore, produced the drawings that constituted the Trident project. Based on a stretched version of the new Grantura chassis, its clean, linear styling and pop-up headlights should have taken TVR on a quantum leap into the realms of grand touring exotica. The project foundered, however, when the company collapsed in the autumn of 1965. This car is chassis number three – restored in 1990 and belonging to Norman Hawkes, who once described it as 'a Griffith 200 with a flashy body'.

The Tridents were to be productionised in glass-fibre. They were fitted with the 271bhp 4.7-litre Ford V8 engine, and since they only weighed about a ton it was no surprise that they could do 150mph. They were shod with Dunlop tyres and 72-spoke 6Jx15 wire wheels, and Alfa Romeo switchgear was used in the wooden dashboard. There were Girling disc brakes all round, and an 18 gallon fuel tank. A pair of fastback-shaped aluminium-bodied Trident prototypes was created at Fissore's workshops in Turin. One went to Jack Griffiths in the States, while the other was shown on the Fissore stand at the 1965 Geneva Show. Here, based on a unit price of $7,790, (£3,362), the Trident attracted orders worth £150,000, on the strength of which it is difficult to see why the business collapsed. In fact part of the problem rested simply on the name of the car – Griffith wanted them to be named after him, and pulled out when Arnold Burton refused to drop the Trident tag with its more prestigious Maserati connotation. The project had cost Grantura Engineering £30,000.

Two further Trident prototypes were made by Fissore in 1965, one a coupé and the other a convertible. Here, its designer Trevor Frost (Fiore) and Martin's father Arthur Lilley pose by the convertible with its top up. When they bought the remains of the TVR concern in November 1965 the Lilleys fondly imagined they were getting the Tridents as well. However, the fibreglass moulds taken from the original Trident prototype had been acquired by Suffolk TVR dealer Bill Last in negotiations involving an out-of-pocket Frost, and Last showed a Trident built up on an Austin-Healey 3000 chassis at the 1966 Racing Car Show at Olympia. Having acquired a stock of Healey chassis and fibreglass bodies from Grantura Plastics, Bill Last eventually went into production with the Trident in 1967, and in various forms it lasted for another decade. Meanwhile the Lilleys prudently decided to concentrate on the traditional TVR series.

A youthful looking Martin Lilley – aged 24 – in the cockpit of the first Trident convertible outside his parents' home at Borehamwood, Hertfordshire. He used this car for about a year until it ceased to have any future as a TVR product. And establishing a precedent for TVR's canine connection, Lilley could be considering whether or not his dog Sandy might have a potential career as a car stylist.

The Trident convertible was bought from John Dobson in 1984 and restored by its present owner Neil Lefley over a lengthy period, and the car is pictured in early 1997 before rewiring and re-trimming took place. Because it is such a rare car the restoration was 'like doing a jigsaw without the picture on the box', according to Lefley. Although it has been repainted pale metallic blue, the car was originally metallic gold.

This is one of Trevor Frost's renderings for a coupé version of the short-lived TVR Tina project. If the provenance is correct, they were done in order to update the original Tina prototypes. Signed by 'Fioré' and dated 1967, the drawings suggest something far more like the Trident, especially in the contours of the roofline, than the reality of the Tina prototypes produced in 1966. They reveal pop-up headlights and driving lamps that the Tina never had, an absence of bumpers, chunkier wheels with centre knock-offs, large-bore twin tail pipes, and a more macho appearance altogether. The rear view seems to indicate a line of cooling vents at the trailing edge of the engine cover.

When Martin Lilley bought the assets of the liquidated Grantura Engineering, TVR bodyshells continued to be made by Grantura Plastics, which had deftly side-stepped the receiver. One of its directors was racer Tommy Entwistle – also president of the TVR Car Club – and in 1967 he designed the Gem with an eye to the next production TVR. It was a slab-fronted aluminium-bodied prototype with a luggage boot, fitted with a Ford Zodiac V6 engine and Ford Capri-style headlights. It used the long wheelbase Tuscan chassis, allied to fully rose-jointed independent wishbone suspension and wide alloy wheels. The aluminium body was replaced by a fibreglass version, retaining the TVR rear screen, and subsequently it received an open front panel, bonnet air scoop and air-dam. It was undeniably graceful from some angles, akin to a Plus 2 Elan perhaps, but the angular front end did it no favours aesthetically.

The car is pictured during the Isle of Man Classic event in 1995 in the paddock with David Hives (of TVR and Grantura Plastics) leaning against it. And as it sits on the grid alongside a Sunbeam Tiger, its purposeful lines leave nothing to the imagination about its intentions.

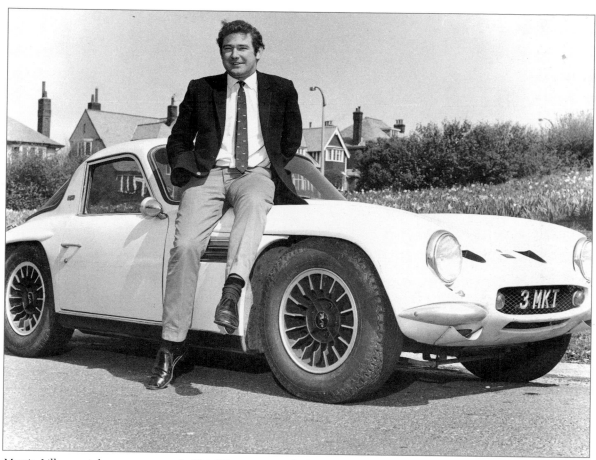

Martin Lilley was always enamoured of big V8 engines, and when he took over at TVR he maintained production of the Griffith, making ten units alongside the MGB-engined Grantura Mark IV 1800S in 1966. Using the same 195bhp engine – and 271bhp rising to 306bhp for the SE version – the Tuscan V8 succeeded the Griffith in 1967, and here he is with his personal transport in '67–'68. Note the little scoops under the front bumpers. The Tuscan's interior specification was of far higher quality than its predecessor's was, and it differed externally from the 1800S in having a bonnet bulge.

At this point in the saga Martin Lilley brought in the longer chassis originally prepared for the Trident, and new, longer doors were fitted in the lengthened bodyshell, and all subsequent Vixens and Tuscans were built on this chassis. Hallmarks of the V8 Tuscan were the pairs of twin bonnet air scoops and a gradual bulge extending back to the scuttle – as distinct from the Griffith, which had a rather abrupt single bump above the pancake air filter. Internally the Tuscan had better quality furniture than the Griffith, with dials set in polished wooden dashboard panels, which differed from its little sister, the contemporary Grantura 1800S. Later the Vixen S2 would adopt the same styling as the Tuscan bonnet – optional at first then standardised.

You could order a Tuscan in one of two specifications. The standard 195bhp model was simply the Tuscan V8, while the 271bhp version was the Tuscan V8SE. The basic model was priced at £1,967 in 1967, which coincided with the E-type Jaguar, and the SE model was £2,363, making it slightly dearer than the E-type 2+2. That was probably too much for a car of the Tuscan's raw character, and of the twenty-eight units made during its one-year production run in 1967, only six remained in the UK. The car pictured is the ex-'Roger Rabbit Racing' Tuscan V8, owned by Paul Weldon, in the paddock at Oulton Park in 1995.

A tale of two Tuscans. To the left is a short-wheelbase car, once owned by Martin Lilley and registered 500 ML, rebuilt 'from a pile of bits' by Neil Lefley and sold to Jeremy Bagnall-Oakley. On the right is PBB 17F, which is a 1967 long-wheelbase Tuscan V8, running the same 289 cu-in Hi Po engine, and used by Lefley as a road car during the 1970s. Both vehicles are finished an attractive burgundy and silver, and the later car has a sunroof, useful for extracting heat and condensation from the cockpit. A contemporary *Motor* magazine road test found that 500ML was the fastest production car to 100mph they had ever tested. By contrast, they also lamented that ventilation was poor, and that valuable luggage space was taken up by the spare wheel.

The Tuscan's top speed was 160mph. Its 271bhp 289 cu-in Hi-Po engine powered it to 100mph in 13.8 seconds, and its 0–60mph time was 5.7 seconds. These stark figures are not half as impressive as the way the Tuscan actually got you there, as its progress was nothing if not dramatic. And brakes were not the efficient items they are today. The engine bay plaque in 500 ML charts the recommended lubricants according to Shell, BP and Castrol, and is headed 'Hoo Hill Works, Layton, Blackpool, England'.

This is a 400bhp Tuscan V8 at high speed at Donington. Its bodywork has been modified to accommodate wider racing rubber, and it was driven by Howard Brearley in thoroughbred and classic events – including the Spa-Francorchamps Six Hours – during the 1990s. Previously painted orange, it is now in white following a massive 140mph seven-car pile-up at Mallory Park in 1996. Howard Brearley had to be cut from the carnage of his totally mangled car, happily uninjured. The Tuscan had a full roll-cage – superior even to FIA standards – built and installed by Phil Stott Performance Engineering of Uttoxeter, Staffordshire, who prepare the car, and it probably saved Brearley's life. However, the Tuscan was rebuilt to perfection by Stott's, with assistance from sponsor Thomas Burberry, and three weeks later it was back in action as this Donington picture demonstrates.

Component supply has always been potentially problematic for small specialist manufacturers, and TVR had to source its MGB engines via local BMC distributors. However, Ford's Industrial Power division offered a direct supply of engines ex-factory, with proper after-sales back-up, and largely for this reason Martin Lilley decided to change power-plants. He introduced the TVR Vixen in 1967 with the Ford 1600 cross-flow engine from the Mark 2 Cortina GT – whose rear lights went on to supersede the old Mark 1 Y-shape variety. Although the Cortina GT unit was slightly less torquey than the MGB engine, it was both lighter, cheaper and a more marketable proposition. TVR Engineering took over construction of the fibreglass bodyshell in 1968, manufactured in the newly acquired premises at Dickies Lane on Marton Moss, and the Vixen S1 was replaced by the longer S2 model. The body was now bolted to the chassis instead of being bonded to it by fibreglass in six sections, which was another important innovation. Pictured at Brands Hatch is a pristine S2 model, belonging to Sarah Millard.

Martin Lilley surveys a trio of S1 Vixens plus a rolling chassis during a tea break at the Hoo Hill factory in 1969. S1s destined for the USA were fitted with the so-called 'sausage' bonnet, which featured a small air intake and bulge extending the length of the bonnet just to the right of centre. This was to accommodate the compressor pump attached to the Ford 1600 engine, which was required to comply with exhaust emissions legislation.

Proud Vixen S2 owner Sarah Millard poses with Martin Lilley beside her car at Brands Hatch in 1997 during the TVR Golden Mania celebrations to mark the company's fiftieth anniversary. By 1969 the Vixen S2 specification had been upgraded to include a Triumph Vitesse differential, servo-assisted braking system and further refinements to the interior like a leather-rim wheel as standard. The single, wide bonnet air-intake of the S1 Vixen had been replaced by an elegant Tuscan-style bulge and a matching pair of shield-shape inlets and extractors beside either end of the hump. The raised area was necessary in order to accommodate an air pump so that the Vixen would comply with the US emissions regulations that were starting to make themselves felt. The mesh grille provided a useful location for the individually fixed licence-plate digits.

In the UK the Vixen cost £1,250 in kit form, or an additional £196 would see it finished at the factory. In 1969 the price was reduced to £1,150 for a Vixen kit to encourage the home market. In fact the model was selling extremely well, with 70 per cent of production going abroad, to the USA, Canada, and Sweden in particular. TVR was back in modest profit, and Lilley was sufficiently confident that he passed on the Racing Car Show and the Motor Show. This is Sarah Millard's immaculate S2 model opposite the pits at Brands Hatch.

Sarah Millard comprehensively restored her Vixen S2 in 1996. Some seventeen layers of earlier pigment were revealed during preparation for its respray, and it is now resplendent in its original red hue, complemented by chrome wire-spoke wheels. The Ford cross-flow engine was rebuilt and fitted with fast road cam, lightened flywheel, machined pistons, and with the single twin-choke Weber carburettor it produces 130bhp.

When North Yorkshire's Croft circuit reopened in 1995, TVR racers had another venue to compete on. This is Martin Barrow's custard yellow Vixen S2, snapped on 27 May 1995 by Steve Beresford. On a minor point of detail, the sidelights and indicators are set into the radiator grille, and the holes in the headlamp nacelles where the sidelights would have been originally have been filled in.

Here is another Vixen campaigner, Paul Rowe, captured at speed by Chris Weaver at Oulton Park during a historic sports/GT race in 1993. This 1970 car is an S3 model, identified by the side indicators located just ahead of the front wheelarches, and the new side air vents sourced from the Ford Zodiac and seen on the subsequent M-series cars. The Vixen S3 differential housing was now from the Triumph GT6 instead of the MGB, and the 86bhp 1599cc Capri 1600GT engine was installed.

In a display that became an automotive industry legend, Martin Lilley went for a big launch for his new M-Series cars and the Zante prototype at the 1971 Earls Court Show. It wasn't just the new chassis that were laid bare. He hired a couple of attractive models, Helen Jones and Susan Shaw, to pose naked with the cars on Pilling Sands near Blackpool, and the photographs were blown up and used as a backdrop for the TVR stand. It was typical of Martin's pioneering streak and (with apologies to that contemporary band The Who – who had a minor hit with Pictures of Lilly) these could indeed be described as Pictures of Lilley's! As a publicity gambit it couldn't have worked better, and on Motor Show press day TVR became the centre of attraction when the girls astonished the world's press by repeating the exercise in person at an unprecedented unveiling ceremony. The car they are adorning in this eve-of-press day shot is a 2500 Vixen.

Vixen S3 braves the snow in the Yorkshire Dales. Since contemporary road tests bemoaned indifferent ventilation and warmth courtesy of the standard issue MGB heater, the occupants presumably dressed accordingly. Like all classic 1960s and '70s TVRs, the Vixen hallmarks included the enormous greenhouse rear window, the Manx tail, modest quarter bumpers, and TVR's own-design alloy wheels that were cast in Birmingham. The Ford 1600-powered Vixen metamorphosed through four evolutions, and the S3 was the second most common. But that's only relative as they were hardly manufactured in large volumes; just 168 Vixen S3s were made between 1970 and 1971, all in kit form, at a price of £1,310. That compares with 117 of the earlier S1 model, 438 units of the S2, and a mere 23 examples of the S4.

Sometime between 1968 and 1970 TVR produced a number of wide-bodied Tuscan V8s. Because records were scanty and many were destroyed in a serious fire at the factory in 1975, there is some question as to how many units were built. These wide-bodied cars were built on a new long-wheelbase chassis, which bore the prefix MAL, and there were several fundamental detail changes in bodywork, light locations and bumper design. They were thus harbingers of the later M-series cars, and in a sense created at a pivotal point in the company's history. This is a contemporary publicity shot featuring TVR's obligatory model girl.

This US car with aftermarket wide-rim Minilite wheels, massive BF Goodrich tyres and twin pairs of tail-pipes is a wide-body Tuscan V8, built in about 1970. The bodyshells for the wide-bodied Tuscan were made in a rented workshop located – ironically – next door to Trevini Plastics, run by none other than Trevor Wilkinson, and each one took as long to make as three regular Vixens. This exceedingly rare model carries a number of hybrid features. It has 2500-style front wing side vents, and the rounded side-window frames found on the subsequent 3000M, and an air vent in the C-pillar. Detailing of the rear panel is also out of step with the contemporary Tuscan V6 and Vixen S2/3, and related to the later M-series models, as are the slight flares over the front wheelarches, and the chrome bumpers. These point to the fact that Martin Lilley was experimenting with fresh design cues for the forthcoming M-series body styling.

According to extensive and detailed research carried out by Illinois-based Guy Dirkin, there were just seven factory-produced Tuscans in this format – broadened by 4 in from the waistline down. This would make them the rarest of all production TVRs. Two further wide-body cars were built up from spare shells on Vixen chassis by TVR Cars of America boss Gerry Sagerman and Liam Churchill at the Barnet Motor Company and fitted with Shelby-Ford Boss 302 cu-in engines. (The latter even had four-wheel drive and a longer chassis and body to match, and in 1998 was being restored by Steve Norgate.) Guy Dirkin owns wide-body Tuscan chassis no. MAL 019, which is fitted with a Holman & Moody-prepared Boss 302 engine that was actually used in the 1970 TransAm series. Mustang fans joke that the engine is worth more than the car, but little do they know! The car illustrated is a beautifully restored wide-body Tuscan V8, chassis number MAL 016, based in Maryland, USA, and now painted metallic brown. When new in 1970 it was finished in white. According to Gerry Sagerman, the first of the wide-bodied Tuscan V8s was finished in early 1970 rather than in 1968 as has been previously supposed. The car he refers to was shown at the New York Motor Show in April 1970, and it was tested by *Road and Track* magazine for its July 1970 issue. The wide-body Tuscan was the last TVR to use a V8 motor until the 350i appeared thirteen years later, and until the 1996 Cerbera GT came out, a wide-body Tuscan running a Boss 302 cu-in engine would have been the fastest TVR ever made.

The mustard-yellow Ford V6-powered Tuscan of Nigel Keeling, right, with Steve Reid's Grantura Mark III outside a fine timber-framed Cheshire inn. In 1970 three TVR models shared the same bodyshell. They were the Tuscan V6, Vixen S2, and the 2500. The Tuscan was powered by Ford's ubiquitous Essex V6 engine, chosen by TVR for pragmatic reasons that included sourcing difficulties with the American V8, availability and cost of the home-grown 3.0-litre Zodiac product, and also it filled the void between 1.6- and 4.7-litre engines. The Vixen outsold the Tuscan V6 by four to one. The Vixen S3 appeared in 1970 using the 1559cc Capri 1600GT unit, and all 165 cars were sold in kit form.

The 3.0-litre Ford V6 Essex engine was a cast-iron unit, fed by a single twin-choke downdraught Weber carb, producing 136bhp at 4750rpm. It had a four-speed gearbox with optional over-drive, and shared the Salisbury differential with the Tuscan V8. To slow it down there were servo-assisted Girling discs at the front and drums at the rear. The air vents in the sides of the front wings were still of the three-slat variety; from 1970 the Tuscan, along with the Vixen S3, would have vents sourced from the Zephyr-Zodiac, and there were now larger side indicators between the front wheelarches and headlights. In 1969 the Tuscan V6 cost £1,492 in kit form, or £1,930 fully built. Because of environmental issues, only seven Tuscan V6s were exported.

This is the rear end of Nigel Keeling's immaculate V6 Tuscan, identified by its badge and up-swept twin tail-pipes. Rear-light clusters are fertile ground for the dedicated TVR anorak: on the Vixen and Tuscan they were mounted on opposite sides (and upside down) to the Cortina Mark 2 they were derived from because of the contours of the Vixen/Tuscan rear quarters. But the new shape of the early M-series cars allowed them to corresponded with the Cortina layout. The mid-period wrap-round M-series rear lights were sourced from the TR6, and those of the later M-series were Lucas items, similar to those used on the Scimitar SE6. From the Vixen S2 through the whole M-series, TVRs used Ford Anglia door hinges that were bolted straight on to suitably thickened fibreglass.

The interior of the Tuscan V6 cockpit is upholstered in black leather and dark grey carpet, relieved by a cream headlining. The dials are laid out in time-honoured format, finished off with a flat leather-rim steering wheel. What may now appear to be rather gloomy and minimalist was considered to be a good, high quality specification back in 1970.

This 1967 Vixen S2 proved to be a very reliable racing car and was campaigned successfully by Nick Parrott in historic sports car events all over South Africa during the mid-1980s on behalf of its owner, John Reid of Reid Readman Racing. The car has a much-modified engine bay, including an aluminium bulkhead and special air filter box. It runs a 175bhp full-race 1650cc Ford motor built by Kent Cams, with a Quaife dog-box and Quaife limited slip diff, and allied to a pair of 45DCOE Weber carburettors and a complex four-branch exhaust manifold. Back at the Blackpool factory, John Reid is TVR's racing team manager, overseeing preparation of the factory cars loaned to guest drivers and the development cars driven by company Chairman and owner Peter Wheeler. The Vixen is now back in the UK and in 1998 was offered for sale in the classified ads in the TVR Car Club's *Sprint* magazine.

Historic racing provides a direct link with TVR's past, as the cars always had a competition background. This is John Reid's 1967 Vixen S2 in the paddock at Kyalami, near Johannesburg, alongside his team's 1971 Lola T212 1798cc Group 6 sports prototype. Driver Nick Parrott notched up numerous victories and Class wins with the Vixen in South African classic events, and on occasions it took the accolade of best-prepared historic sports car in the country.

By 1967 environmental controls were starting to become a serious issue in the all-important North American market, and the Tuscan's V6 Ford engine could not pass emissions tests. Therefore when the Tuscan V6 was barely a year old, Martin Lilley was pressured to find an eligible engine. He settled on the straight-six 2500 Triumph unit with Stromberg carburettors, used in the 1967 TR250 or TR5, and the TR6. At 106bhp/4900rpm, it lacked the power and torque of the Ford V6 motor, but at least it was fully certified and supply was guaranteed by Triumph's new status as part of the British Leyland conglomerate. The engine and TR6 gearbox was mounted in the standard 1.5in diameter 16-gauge multi-tubular Vixen S3/Tuscan chassis, where the Triumph differential was also housed. It ran on Tuscan 5.5in wheels, and to comply with fuel evaporation regulations it had a smaller fuel tank than its siblings. The model was known as the TVR 2500 Vixen, and was first shown at the 1970 Earls Court Show. A fourth Vixen-bodied model, the TVR 1300, was made between 1971 and 1972 using the 1296cc Triumph Spitfire engine. Just fifteen units were made with this engine, nine on the old chassis and six on the new M-chassis. This is a 2500 of 1971, belonging to Bernie Hartnett, snapped with a Spitfire Mk V at RAF Coningsby, Lincolnshire. The Minilite wheels look good.

The 2500 Vixen model was only ever available in Stromberg carburettor form rather than with TR5 injection, so it was not much quicker than a Vixen S3. However, in 1971 TVR made 237 units of the 2500 model against 97 Vixen S3s, with a further 44 of the six-cylinder Triumph-powered cars produced in early 1972 prior to the new 'M' chassis coming on stream. The new M-series bodyshell had yet to be finalised, and another 95 hybrid 2500s appeared later that year, their M-chassis clad with Vixen S3-type bodywork, and more refined interior. Most TVR 2500s went to the States, and meanwhile, back in Blackpool, along with productionising the new 2500 model, it was a busy time for the company in other respects too. The start of the new decade marked a turning point in TVR's history, as the whole operation relocated over the 1970 Christmas holiday from Hoo Hill to new premises at Bristol Avenue. This plant was formerly the home of Busma caravans, and prior to that it was a cutlery factory; TVR remains there to this day. The new body shop was built at the rear of the factory in 1972, with body-building and painting equipment transferring from Marton Moss. The new service bay was constructed alongside in 1976. Pictured having fun at Lodge Corner, Oulton Park, during a TVR Car Club track day in 1996, is the 2500 of Bernie Hartnett, followed by the Grantura Mark III of Ian Massey-Cross.

With the Thurner-designed chassis now some nine years old – with a single lengthening of the wheelbase to 7ft 6in in 1967 – the time was ripe for a new chassis. It was designed by Martin Lilley and Midlands TVR dealer Mike Bigland during 1971, and the first of the new M-series cars was a 2500M, announced at the salacious 1971 Earls Court Show. The M-chassis heralded a new boom-time at TVR, which would endure right through the 1970s. Once the logistics of bringing the diverse operations that made the various components on to one site had been rationalised, output progressed from eight to ten cars a week by late 1972. Just over half of production was exported to the USA, as well as to new markets including Japan, Germany, Cyprus and Greece. In 1972 a shortage of the TVR alloy wheels prompted the fitting of steel rims.

The new M-chassis was based on proposals from engineer Mike Bigland, who had a TVR dealership at Halesowen and went on to become TVR's technical director, and who advocated beefing up the chassis by using a mixture of square and round section tubing. This one was photographed at the factory for publicity purposes in 1972, and shows the mixture of 1.5in 14- and 16-gauge square- and round-section tubing.

The fibreglass bodyshell was bolted to the chassis through rubber mountings, and a residue of machine oil went some way to providing an internal anti-corrosion coating. The finished chassis was then given a coat of synthetic rubber sealant before the body was fitted. Several of the body mounting points can be seen, on the front subframe, the rear platform and brackets at the corners of the outriggers. Although the handbrake lever is present, the gearlever would be fitted only after the body was mounted. Behind, a completed car waits with its forward hinged bonnet up, a couple of rows of engines are ready for installation, and a contemporary kitsch poster of General Kitchener exhorts the workforce to 'clean up'. It must have worked, as it all looks pretty tidy in the photograph.

The suspension was independent all round, consisting of unequal length wishbones, coil springs and dampers, plus front anti-roll bar. Steering was by rack and pinion. The cast-iron 2498cc straight-six Triumph motor sits well back in the chassis for optimum weight distribution, and is coupled to a five-speed all-synchromesh Triumph gearbox. Some models used Zenith carbs, while Strombergs remained most common fitment.

The TVR 2500M used the new M-chassis ('M' stood for Martin) and featured a greatly revised bodyshell. It was 9in longer than the Vixen/Tuscan, most of which was present in the front overhang. This enabled the spare wheel to be located ahead of the engine, which liberated the platform in the tail for luggage space. There were now much more prominent chrome bumpers, and the rear light clusters were sourced from the TR6. Performance of the 2500M was by no means startling, given that the standard European spec Triumph TR6 engine was good for 125mph. In US Federal form the 2500M could achieve a maximum of only 109mph, with 0–60mph coming up in a modest 9.3 seconds. When it was shown at the 1972 New York Auto Show there was not too much interest, and Gerry Sagerman concluded that a V8 engine was needed to make it a viable proposition in the States. The car weighed a ton exactly, and power output from the straight-six engine was a somewhat lowly 106bhp at 4900rpm. Compensations included an overdrive, optional sunroof, heated rear 'greenhouse', a laminated windscreen, tinted glass, and in fact the overall specification and build quality placed it well above its predecessors in real terms.

The new body was more than a simple facelift. The 2500M received comprehensive new frontal treatment, including the relocation of indicators and sidelights to the sides of the radiator grille aperture, which gave a clean line to the headlight nacelles. There were now longer and perhaps more elegant chromed quarter bumpers that produced a more mature look for the car. The front aperture was deliberately enlarged to access more air for the de-smogged 2498cc straight six, which was otherwise prone to overheat, and a new cross-flow radiator was installed. All the M-series range used identical shells, with the sculpted panel down the centre of the bonnet flanked by a single air intake on either side. The traditional TVR design was further rationalised so that the lip over the rear wheelarch now disappeared. However, only the 2500M retained the air vents in the front wings.

Classic TVRs are by now likely to be in need of restoration, and this 2500M is a typical example of a relatively straightforward job. It belongs to Craig Polly, who completed a full restoration in 1997 largely on his own, having owned the car for twelve years. It is a 1972 model, chassis 2254TM, making it the fourteenth car in the series. Preparation for the respray took a whole year. Craig began by scraping off several layers of paint by hand, after which he attended to general and widespread crazing of the gel coat, grinding out crazed areas and renewing with fibreglass mat and resin. After renewing the bonnet frame a local firm repainted the car in tartan red over a two-month period. The TVR alloy wheels were laboriously paint-stripped, shotblasted and powdercoated black. During this time Craig had the seats and trim panels re-upholstered, and a new headlining was made up on the domestic sewing machine. Meanwhile, he refurbished the mechanical ancillaries. The engine (right), was simply repainted, but the gearbox and overdrive was overhauled. The chassis was sufficiently good that a fresh coat of paint was all that was required. New wheel bearings, suspension bushes, track-rod ends and universal joints were renewed, while new brake pipes, callipers, pads and shoes, fuel lines and radiator hoses were fitted. Apart from the idiosyncrasies of classic TVR motoring – relatively primitive now compared with modern cars, Craig enjoys using his car during the summer months, when the inadequacies of the heating system are not a problem.

The Triumph-engined TVR 2500 model was conceived as an export vehicle, and went on to become TVR's strongest seller for five years, with 947 units sold between 1972 and 1977. This picture shows preparations around the cargo hold of an Irish International aircraft to dispatch one of the very first Vixen/Tuscan bodied 2500s to North America to be tested for the stringent US emissions tests. Between 1972 and 1973 twenty-three units of the Vixen S4 were also produced on the M-chassis, their specification otherwise identical to the S3.

This pristine yellow 3000M has returned to Blackpool for the 'Back Home' event in 1992. This model was produced between 1972 and 1979, during which period 654 units were produced with normally aspirated 3.0-litre Ford V6 Essex engines. Top speed was 125mph and 0–60mph time was 7.7 seconds. An upmarket version known as the 3000ML with more luxurious cabin was introduced in 1973. That year, the specialist car industry was rocked to its foundations with the introduction of VAT (Value Added Tax) on kit cars, which meant that there was no financial incentive for customers to build cars themselves.

Interiors of the M-series cars were finished to a very high standard, although some people thought the driving position was an acquired taste. This is actually the even more sumptuous ML interior, which has a walnut veneer dashboard fascia, leather-sided high-back seats with built in head restraints, leather piping to the carpeting, and leather cladding for the scuttle top, leather-bound steering wheel rim, gearlever and handbrake boots. Ventilation outlets are on the scuttle top and face, while windows are wound up and down by hand. Instrument dials are clustered behind the steering wheel, with period radio and heater controls in the centre, plus rocker switches and ashtray on the typically broad console over the transmission tunnel. The tops of the door window frames have a more rounded finish than the previous models.

A typical early M-series TVR in the paddock at Donington Park during the TVR Car Club's Extravaganza meeting. It was virtually impossible to distinguish the 2500M from the 3000M externally as they shared the same bodyshell. Exhaust pipes usually gave the game away, as 3000M tail pipes were far apart, while those of the 2500M were siamesed. After-market systems confuse the issue, however. Around 1976 the M-series chrome bumpers were replaced by black foam-filled rubber absorbent bumpers. The 1970s were a period of stability at TVR, because production problems had been eliminated and the uniformity of body style and the excellent M-series chassis brought good sales. Yet three critical events threatened to harm the company. After the demise of the kit car industry the UK was beset by a three-day working week in 1973, owing to the oil crisis, precipitating component shortages. TVR kept up production by importing a huge generator to provide power and light for the factory. Strikes were rife in the '60s and '70s, but perhaps the most crucial was the delay in supply of Triumph engines because of a strike at the Canley factory. The third shock was the mysterious factory fire, possibly caused by an electrical fault in a car, in January 1975, which destroyed the main assembly block, devastated cars in build and halted production completely. Martin Lilley caught pneumonia straight afterwards, but by the Earls Court Motor Show in October the firm was back on its feet once more.

By 1973 TVRs were being marketed in the Netherlands by enterprising specialists, and the factory began to have specifications related to production years from 1974, governed by the US market, which began in the October. Although something like 80 per cent of production was orientated towards North America, the push into mainland Europe also started in 1974. This suspension detail comes from a Dutch 3000M. It belongs to Hubert Leferink, who has been restoring the car since 1995, inspired by his friend's 1979 model. The hub carrier is cast with the lettering TVR Eng. Ltd, 6-73, indicating the part was manufactured in June 1973. The body is being painted sunset yellow.

Newly refurbished Ford 3.0-litre Essex V6 engine installed in the pristine 3000M chassis of Hubert Leferink. The engine is painted blue, while cam covers are chromed, and where appropriate, ancillaries have been highly polished or painted silver or white to match. All pipe runs are new, in what is obviously a first-class restoration.

This shot of the 3000M chassis on the 1973 motor show stand is well lit, and shows clearly the geometry of the chassis and suspension pick-up points, as well as the neat pipe runs. The rectangular box structure carries the differential and rear suspension, while the outriggers provide the platform for the bodyshell, and the tubular spine that expands towards the front of the car carries the drive train, and neatly cradles the V6 motor. This is a neat fit, located well behind the front axle line, and the forward mounting of the spare wheel above the radiator frees up luggage space in the cabin, although weight transfer is altered in the process. Note the semi-circular upper wishbone and lower triangulated item. By 1975 these items would be zinc-plated.

With bodyshell fitted, the housing of the ancillaries in the 3000M's engine bay such as battery and fluid reservoirs is clear. Access to the spare wheel under the forward-hinged bonnet is no less difficult than extracting it from behind the seats in earlier models, but the installation is preferable. At lower right inside the cabin, air vents directed at the windscreen can be seen in the top of the dashboard padding.

The main assembly area at the Bristol Avenue factory in the early '70s, with a collection of Vixen/Tuscan-type 2500s in build. A number of straight-six powertrains have been installed in pre-M-series chassis. The assembly line clearly has some way to go before it metamorphosed into the more disciplined – and crowded – operation it had become by the 1990s. The administration offices are at the far end of the workshop.

Here is another view of the main assembly area in the early 1970s, showing the 2500s being constructed. At the right of the picture is a stack of round-tube chassis fresh from the welding shop and to the left a pile of steel rods and oxygen bottles. Beyond the far side of the assembly area is production stores, delineated by component storage bins and tea chests, with a few bucket seats and tyres on racks. The handy pillar-mounted fire extinguishers would have been useful, had anybody been there to use them, when the whole of the central block was gutted by fire on the evening of 3 January 1975.

The Zante – named after a Greek island – was styled by Harris Mann (who later styled the TR7), made by the Huntingdon-based firm Specialised Mouldings and was at first known as the TVR SM. Although it used the old Thurner chassis when shown at the notorious 1971 Earls Court Show – when its creator Peter Jackson was slapped for trying to remove a naked woman from its sagging roof – it would have been the first TVR prototype body to use the Bigland-designed M-chassis. The dramatically upswept tail culminated in a rear tailgate, which would have been a first for the company. But for broadly financial reasons Martin Lilley decided not to productionise it; for one thing, Gerry Sagerman was not enthusiastic about its prospects in the States. However, it demonstrates that Lilley was considering a design not dissimilar in concept to the Tasmin a full decade before TVR went wedge shape, and was ahead of the Lotus Type 75 Elite style-wise by three years.

The staff of TVR poses outside the Bristol Avenue administration block behind a row of brand new M-series models in 1974. Martin Lilley is just to the left of the only car to have a registration plate. By 1975 the 3000M and 1600M had dispensed with the air intakes on the bonnet and front wing sides, although the 2500M ran hotter and retained them. In 1973 an upmarket version of the 3000M was introduced, known as the 3000ML. The extra £300 bought a cloth roof lining, Wilton carpets and a walnut dashboard fascia, plus specially designed 6J x 14 alloy wheels.

The lower end of the engine capacity market was catered for by the Spitfire-powered 1300M and Ford Kent-powered 1600M. Just fifteen cars were made with the little Triumph engine, which in any case was a cross-over model with Vixen-type bodywork and only six built on the M-chassis, but the 1600M was a pukka M-series car and demand was a bit stronger, although hardly overwhelming. Between 1972 and 1977 a mere 148 units were produced. It used the 1599cc cast-iron Ford Kent engine coupled to a four-speed gearbox with overdrive, fed by a single twin-choke Weber carburettor, and developed 84bhp at 5500rpm. This is Stan Cook's car, snapped on the Isle of Man. Registration number MRN 844P, it is the actual car featured by *Autocar* magazine in its upbeat road test of 3 April 1976. They concluded that the 1600M is a good stepping stone for those who cannot manage a 'big' TVR. Stan Cook has retrimmed the interior in dark blue, removed the vinyl roof and fitted Wolfrace wheels, but everything else is original.

Ready for the off on the grid at Mallory Park short circuit in 1976, with Chris Alford's 1600M on pole position. Opposition consists of a couple of MGBs, a Morgan, an assortment of Spridgets and a Ginetta G15. Three rows back is a Grantura, bearing the traditional 'Le Mans'-style shield-shaped cooling vents on its bonnet. The Kenlowe engine-cooling fan is prominent behind a mesh grille at the front of Alford's 1600M's engine, and the sidelights have been covered over.

One of the most successful TVR racers of the mid-1970s was classic racing car dealer Chris Alford, who had a fair measure of successes driving Morgans as well. There is a hint of wheelspin as Chris Alford drops the clutch of the 1600M to get off the line at Mallory Park at a round of the 1976 Shellsport prodsports championship. The TVR's Ford Kent powerplant was prepared by Dartford-based Minister engines who specialised in tuning engines for the highly competitive Formula Ford category, while the car was run by TVR and Morgan dealer John Britten's Arkley Garage.

Chris Alford takes the Britten Garage's 'All British Racing Team' 1600M past the apex of Brands Hatch's Graham Hill Bend ahead of a Morgan 4/4 and an MGB in a production sports cars race in 1976. Being traditional sports cars, Morgans were always going to run the TVRs close, while the essentially roadgoing MGB was at a disadvantage weight-wise as well as requiring a lot more specialist setting up to make it handle as well as the other two.

Chris Alford rounds the Mallory Park hairpin in 1977 in the re-liveried 1600M. The optional Taimar stripe around the car's waist was an instant hit, and John Britten's Arkley Garage was quick to promote it with a view to boosting sales of the new model.

During the 1960s and 1970s a number of people developed and raced TVRs, mainly Griffiths and Tuscans. They included Peter Simpson and Dudley Hardwicke, David Plumstead – of Mongoose fame, Martin Bolsover, Gerry Marshall in Martin Lilley's Barnet Motor Company Griffith MMT 7C, which was subsequently written off twice, firstly by autocross expert John Akers and again after a rebuild by circuit racer Gillian Fortescue-Thomas. One of the most significant racing cars was Richard Taft's 4.7-litre Tuscan, which was based on a more robust chassis built in 1971 by Mike Bigland, and it was this creation that went on to spawn the M-series chassis. Other names of note were Ed Stevens, Maurice Gates, Rod Gretton, Chris Meek and Colin Blower, while Modsports champions in TVRs included Rod Longton and Brian Hough, but the latter was killed at Thruxton in 1973 – in the ex-Taft car – when in sight of a third title. The Tuscan-based hillclimb version illustrated here exemplifies the Modsports TVR with its massively flared front and rear wheelarches, front air dam and pop-riveted windscreen. It runs a 4.7-litre Ford V8 engine, and by the late 1980s it had been further modified by its owner Paul Tankard with side exhausts and rear aerofoils.

Calm before the storm on the TVR stand at the Frankfurt Motor Show, 1977, organised by the German concessionaire Gert Coerper of Dusseldorf. The two cars on display are 3000Ms, with the basic model on the left and the more expensive ML luxury version with special paintwork and interior and Wolfrace wheels on the right.

Martin Lilley, left, had an eye for a marketing coup, and engaged Niki Lauda to sign autographs on the TVR stand at the 1977 Frankfurt Show. Only the previous year the Austrian had been gravely injured in the German Grand Prix, and such was his amazing recovery that he was to be World Champion for the second time in 1977. Success breeds success, and meanwhile the new TVR Taimar hatchback was waiting in the wings.

The Taimar was the culmination of the M-series coupés, as the entire rear screen lifted up as a hatchback. It was hinged at the front, with hinges at either corner of the roof, and the gas struts that supported it were so strong that they penetrated the fibreglass of the window surround. The release button was concealed above the lock in the right-hand-side doorjamb, and clearly it could only be accessed when the door was open. It was a logical innovation to make, and in fact the hatchback facility had been under discussion since the early 1970s. At last owners could stash their luggage via the hatch instead of heaving it over the seats. However, panel fit was not always completely accurate, and an efficient seal is essential to ensure exhaust fumes are not sucked back inside the car. The Taimar's colour scheme normally featured the contrasting band around its flanks. It was slightly heavier than the 3000M, at 2,260lb against 2,240lb, and for obvious reasons it was also a dearer car. When both models were discontinued in 1980, the Taimar cost £7,211, while the 3000M cost £6,417. During its three-year production run 395 normally aspirated Taimars were built, with 15 made in the autumn of 1976, but 155 completed the following year when it proved more popular than the 3000M, of which 132 units were made. This low angle shot of the Taimar is a TVR publicity photograph, taken in 1977, with sunroof open.

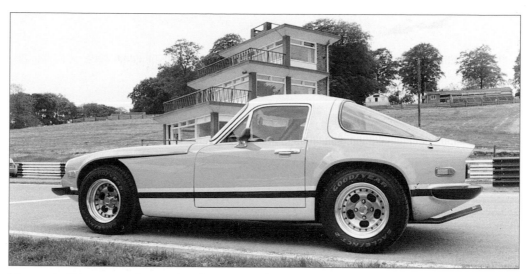

The regular Taimar was a fine car, but the Taimar Turbo was an exceptional one. This red and gold Taimar Turbo sits on the grid at Cadwell Park during a TVR Car Club track day in June 1995.

Turbocharging was relatively new in production cars at the time, and although the concept dated back to First World War aircraft – the extra power enabled planes to gain altitude and escape anti-aircraft fire – the technology had only been applied to cars by Chevrolet, BMW, Saab and Porsche. The Taimar Turbo was first seen at Earls Court in 1975 – adorned by a pair of bare-breasted girls swathed in Men Only sashes.

In 1976 TVR was the only British manufacturer to offer a turbo, and it was applied first to the 3000M, of which twenty cars were turbocharged. Of the Taimar Turbo, thirty were produced between 1976 and 1979, and for the most part they were right-hand drive machines. The 3.0-litre V6 Essex engine breathed through a twin-choke Weber carburettor, and the exhaust-driven Holset or Garrett AiResearch turbochargers were sourced from Broadspeed Engineering who had developed the application in the early '70s. Were the body graphics over the top? Well yes, just so there was no possibility of confusing the Turbo version with any other Taimar. This is the metallic grey 1978 car, with Wolfrace wheels, belonging to Vasco and Tracie Carter, chassis number 4279FM.

The interior of the Taimar Turbo looked more conventional and, understandably, less opulent than the SE. This is Vasco Carter's 1978 car, with a four-spoke steering wheel and clocks and instrumentation ranged broadly horizontally just below eye level, amid an ocean of padded black leathercloth.

This Taimar Turbo SE has a 'Moonroof' sunroof, and the interior is trimmed with brown Wilton carpet throughout, and it has a mohair headlining, a walnut dashboard and full oatmeal leather upholstery. The creature comforts extend to the four-speaker National Panasonic stereo system with built-in graphic equaliser mounted above the rear view mirror. There is an electric aerial, Selmar burglar alarm, map reading light, electric windows and door mirrors, air conditioning and a clock. This was quite an exceptional specification in 1979, even for TVRs, which never stinted on the essentials.

The engine of the Taimar Turbo SE is a turbocharged 3.0-litre Ford V6 'Essex' unit with the Broadspeed developed turbo installation. It is balanced and blueprinted, and develops 230bhp, giving a top speed of 145mph and 0-60mph acceleration time of 5.5 seconds. The turbocharger itself is housed low down and to the front of the engine, and the reversed manifolds feed the exhaust gasses to spin the turbine that connects with the pressurised plenum chamber on top of the downdraught Weber carburettor.

Vinyl roofs and matching side-stripes were the order of the day for these 2500Ms lined up outside the Bristol Avenue plant in 1977.

This Taimar Turbo SE is owned by Mr R. Purdell and is one of only four factory-built Turbo SEs – three were Taimars and the fourth was a convertible. The lavish SE specification includes a bodyshell widened with flared wheelarches to accommodate its split-rim Compomotive wheels and 205/60 tyres, but the real luxury treatment is in the cabin fittings and furnishings. Mr Purdell has all the original TVR invoices and European market warranty documentation that reveals it to be chassis number FM4537. It was first registered on 20 June 1979, and cost £14,250.

Fans of the BBC radio soap drama *The Archers* will be delighted to know that next door to The Bull is an equally august institution, although perhaps more familiar to aficionados of classic TVRs. The Worcestershire village of Inkberrow, alias Ambridge, is the home of David Gerald Sportscars, who took over the supply and manufacturing rights of all pre-1980 TVRs in 1987. They struck a £2m deal with the factory to obtain all the jigs to produce complete chassis and suspension systems, together with the master bucks and body moulds to manufacture brand new shells. Proprietor Gerry Jinks – the Gerald of David Gerald – has built up the business to include a restoration workshop where early models receive comprehensive ground-up restorations, and there are always a dozen or so examples in stock. Prominent in the showroom is a 3000S convertible, one of only 108 made in right-hand drive. The car was later bought by Roger Baines. David Gerald also carries a vast quantity of spares for these models, and during the 1990s the firm specialised in finding and importing Griffiths from the United States.

A collection of spare Vixen and M-series bucks and bonnet moulds behind the workshops of classic TVR specialist David Gerald Sportscars. Customers needing new panels or a full or partial restoration need look no further for the wherewithal and the expertise to get the job done (telephone 01386 793237).

The 3000S Convertible was the final model in the M-series range. In production form it was a first for
TVR, since everything from Grantura onwards had been a coupé. It used the familiar M-series chassis,
and the front section of the body was the same as the regular M-series cars, but from the scuttle back the
Convertible was a fresh design. The windscreen surround was specially made, and the doors with their
distinctive dished top, together with the boot and the car's entire rear quarters, were all new.
Considerable thought and application went into the new engineering required to make a convertible,
including the retractable soft-top. The Convertible's side windows were opened by sliding the sections
either backwards or forwards, and could be removed altogether if necessary. The side-impact beams
within the doors ruled out roll-up window mechanism in those days. It can be seen how the rear bootlid
deck of the 3000S is undercut by the car's rear panel to form a neat spoiler. This is a Belgian car with
split-rim Compomotive wheels and rollover hoop outside the pits garages at Zolder circuit.

During the last two years of M-series production, there was more demand for the 3000S than either of
the other mainstream models: TVR made 258 convertibles in 1978 and 1979, against 225 Taimars and
80 3000Ms during the same period. When production ended in 1980 the 3000S cost £8,730. Of the
63 turbocharged M-series cars, 13 Convertibles used the forced induction method, and all were produced
in right-hand-drive form. With full tonneau cover fitted, this is a 3000S Turbo in the Donington Park
paddock for the TVR Extravaganza meeting.

Under-bonnet shot of this 3000S Turbo does little to identify the actual turbocharger, which is tucked away to the lower front right of the 3.0-litre Ford Essex V6 engine. Only the pressurised plenum chamber above the Weber carburettor and the pipe that feeds it are visible. Like its sister car, the Taimar Turbo, the 3000S Turbo develops 230bhp, giving a top speed of 145mph and 0–60mph acceleration time of 5.5 seconds.

This is a 3000S Convertible with a difference, as it runs a full-house 5.0-litre V8 engine. It belongs to Dave Smith and is being put through its paces at the TVR Car Club's National Track Day at Silverstone, on 1 September 1995. One neat solution to the location of that tiresome UK numberplate can be seen here: it has been relegated to the car's lower air intake.

A delighted looking Martin Lilley relives a bit of TVR history that he created, seen here at Brands Hatch during the Golden Mania celebrations in 1997. This 3000S is the only SE-spec Convertible ever made, and Martin Lilley used it as his own transport for eighteen months when it carried the factory plate TVR 100, before registering it and selling it on. Today this unique car belongs to Stewart McCarte who acquired it in 1993. Like the Taimar Turbo SE, the Convertible SE has extended wheelarches to accommodate the Compomotive split-rim wheels, a limited slip differential, leather upholstered interior and an exclusive dashboard.

Dutchman Hubert Leferink runs a TVR S2 and in 1998 had nearly completed the restoration of a 3000M. He and his friend already have their next project in hand, which is this 1978 Convertible 3000S. It had an interesting history, having spent its early years in Zaire, and for climatic reasons apparently never had a heater fitted. Its windscreen was perspex, and had been replaced every three months or so because the strong sunlight rendered it opaque. The car came to the Netherlands via Belgium.

CHAPTER THREE

THE WEDGE ERA

The idea was good but the timing was out. When Martin Lilley elected to devote TVR production entirely to the new wedge-shaped Tasmin, a financial crisis loomed that would in effect see him hand over the keys to Peter Wheeler and walk away. The wedge era lasted for a decade, however, and the cars grew ever more brash, culminating in the mighty 420SEAC.

Discreet TVR badging and personalised numberplate mark out Peter Fisher's 350i as a well-cared-for car, which has the 1985 streamlined wing mirrors. The wedge era that spanned the 1980s is generally notable for being a time of sports convertible production — or at least the second half of the decade — as opposed to the coupés that TVR's reputation was based on in the 1960s and '70s. However, a small number of coupés were built with the Rover V8 power unit — 52 between 1983 and 1987, against 650 of the 350i Convertibles made during the same period. In 1983 and 1984 they also made six units of the 350i as +2 coupés.

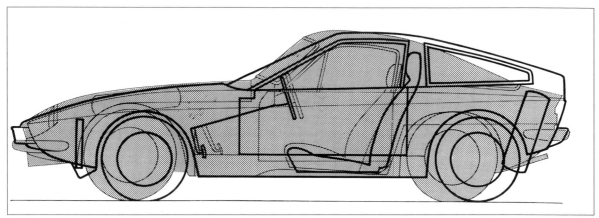

The late 1970s and early '80s were not a good time for traditional sports and GT cars, with a combination of market factors, corporate meddling and growing environmental pressure taking stale old designs like the MGB V8, Spitfire, and not so old TR7/8 out of production. Martin Lilley saw a widening niche in the market for a new, slightly more prestigious model, and although the wedge shape was by no means new, it was still very much topical – see contemporary Lotus Esprit, Alfetta GTV, Ferrari 308GTS and Fiat X1/9 for example. And after all, TVR had been there first with its 1971 Zante prototype. The proportions of the first series Tasmin were quite different to those of the M-series car, as this factory overlay shows. The wheelbase is longer, and the cabin is more spacious with potentially greater distance between driver's seat and controls, although the rake of the windscreen is much steeper. The Tasmin coupé provides greater luggage space, and the spare wheel is mounted below the rear hatch for better access.

The wind of change began to blow at Blackpool in 1979, with Martin Lilley's decision to drop the traditional TVR shape that he had nurtured for thirteen years and replace it with a completely new model. The Tasmin – named not after a fictitious girlfriend, but rather with an eye to the Antipodean 'Tasman' Formula 2 series – was designed in 1977 by Oliver Winterbottom, who had penned the Lotus Elite 501 and Eclat 520 that were launched in 1974/5. He had previously worked in Jaguar's drawing office, moving on to become styling manager at Lotus. The similarities between TVR and Lotus models – particularly the Eclat – were clear, but the proportions of the Tasmin placed the cabin further back on the bodyshell. This is an S1 model belonging to TVR Car Club member J. Burnham.

Development of the Tasmin took over three years, involving an investment of £500,000 in new jigs, machine tools and moulds and the necessary revision of space at the factory, as well as setting up a development shop at nearby Preston. Not only did the Tasmin stylist come from Lotus, but also its chassis draughtsman was another exile from Hethel, Ian Jones, who drew up the chassis and running gear for the new TVR. The tubular spaceframe chassis was similar to that of the M-series, composed of 1.5in-diameter 14-gauge steel tubes, but differed in many aspects of detail, broadening out at the engine bay and dispensing with the rectangular rear section that previously accommodated the differential. Not surprisingly, the Tasmin's suspension system was similar to that of the Lotus wedges, comprising Ford Cortina and Granada suspension componentry for its wishbone independent front and semi-trailing arms with transverse link at the rear with inboard disc brakes. Within a year from the launch of the Tasmin S1 Coupé came the Convertible, which had a revised windscreen surround and of course came with a bootlid and soft-top, as well as up-swept door tops. This is a TVR press picture of the Tasmin S1 on the Blackpool promenade. In a similar way to the Lotus wedges, the fibreglass bodyshell of the Tasmin was moulded in two halves and bonded across the car's waistline – the graphics show whereabouts the actual join was – and it was mounted on the outrigger sections of the tube-frame chassis. Bumpers were made of fibreglass, and the front section could be removed for replacement if necessary. The specification included laminated Sundym windscreen, toughened glass side and rear windows, while the interior was upholstered in shades of 'chestnut with caviar' velour or fake leather. The dashboard was panelled in walnut veneer, and there was a full range of instrumentation and accessories as standard.

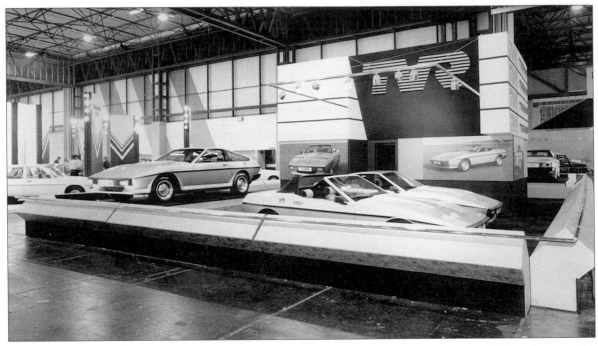

Eve of press day at the NEC in October 1980 for the launch of the new range of TVRs. Featured models are the Tasmin S1 Coupé and the new Convertible and Plus Two (+2) Coupé models. They were undoubtedly well received, but the major change in production meant that whereas TVR sold 308 cars in 1979, only 144 orders were taken in 1980. A more positive milestone passed late in 1980 was the production of the 5,000th TVR – a Tasmin.

Martin Lilley greets the Duke of Gloucester on the TVR stand at the NEC in 1980. The company's marketing campaign was based around the 'Battle for Britain' slogan, which Lilley perceptively championed in the face of growing Japanese and Continental opposition. The Tasmin was £3,000 dearer than the outgoing Taimar, which was a significant sum even then. Martin Lilley had wanted to market the Tasmin at a lower price, but the cash flow forecasts necessary to placate the financial institutions would not allow it. The abrupt switch to an all-new model range happened for two reasons. Much of the major componentry for the M-series cars was sourced from the out-of-production TR6, and its manufacturers declined to continue making obsolete parts. And supplies of those Mk II Consul windscreens were drying up. In addition, impending crash and safety regulations would have required the M-series to be redesigned, and like the E-type Jaguar, its forward-hinged bonnet alone needed a radical re-think.

The new models were powered by a new engine as well. The Ford 'Essex' V6 that had featured in the M-series cars was replaced by the 2792cc German Cologne-built Ford V6 unit that had first appeared in the Granada in 1977, and the internal dimensions of its cast-iron block were completely different to its predecessor. Gone was the downdraught Weber, and in came state-of-the-art Bosch K-Jetronic fuel injection, which helped lift power output to 160bhp at 5700rpm. The non-overdrive Capri/Granada four-speed gearbox was the same as that fitted to M-series models, however, although the expanding Tasmin range was available with automatic transmission from October 1980. This is a 1981 Tasmin S1 Convertible.

The end of the old regime came towards the end of 1981, when Martin Lilley was overtaken by financial difficulties. Not only were the new cars slow to take off, but TVR was still reeling from a contretemps with the US customs over the documentation for twenty-five 3000Ss. These vehicles had been impounded in 1978 and TVR never received the £287,500 they represented. And the Tasmin could not be sold in the potentially lucrative US marketplace because its German Ford V6 engine was not yet de-toxed. TVR was refused state aid – which had been liberally dished out to British Leyland and Chrysler ten years earlier – and negotiations with businessman and shareholder Peter Wheeler saw the Lilley epoch draw to a close.

The Tasmin remained in production,
however, and early cars have a small
but significant following today,
representing probably the cheapest
way into the secondhand TVR
market. Here is Ian Maddox
having fun at the 1996 Oulton Park
Track Day.

The TVR Press Office has always been hot on publicity pictures, and this shot of the Tasmin 200 Convertible is typically clear and posed somewhere in the wilds of Cumbria or the Trough of Bowland north-east of Preston. This model was produced between 1981 and 1984, along with a Coupé version. And while it shared the same bodyshell and suspension componentry as the Tasmin S2 models, it was powered by the 1993cc four-cylinder Ford ohc Pinto engine found in the Capri and Cortina 2000s, and mated to the Ford four-speed gearbox. As an entry-level TVR it lacked a few refinements of the bigger-engined Tasmins, like electric windows and radio cassette player, although the BBS alloys are an improvement on the standard issue TVR wheels. It didn't sell well, however, and only 45 Tasmin 200 Convertibles and 16 Coupés were made.

The factory numberplate was applied to a number of demonstrators, and this is a 1982 Tasmin Convertible with pop-up headlights raised. A total of 812 units were made between 1980 and 1986, most successful year being 1985 when 239 left the factory. The company made an important step in 1983 when it began selling cars to the United States again. This was made possible because of the Cologne 2.8-litre engine being de-smogged by the rigorous German TUV inspectorate, but with catalytic converter fitted, power output was down to 145bhp. US cars were also subjected to the indignity of carrying massive impact-absorbing bumpers fore and aft, so they weighed some 300lb more than European-spec models.

One innovative aspect of the Tasmin Convertible was the rollover hoop or rear header that doubled as part of the hood support. It could be kept erect in the upright position, or folded back along with the soft-top, and the electric windows retracted, to create the full sports car effect. This 1982 car has the later fuel cap flap, while other parts sourced from the Ford parts bin include the Capri rear-light clusters and door handles. The Tasmin used Cortina rack and pinion steering, but the switchgear mounted on the steering column came from British Leyland. Probably no other car has such a steeply inclined windscreen as the Tasmin; it comes almost over the top of the occupants' heads.

For the first time in its history (not counting Trevor Wilkinson's RGS Atalanta sports saloons), TVR made a concession to two-plus-two family motoring with the Plus Two model in 1980. While recognisably a Tasmin, the Plus Two (+2) version was different in several important respects. It was three inches longer than the two-seater cars, and although the doors were identical, the nose of the +2 was shorter, the bonnet moulding was entirely different and the louvres were absent. The front spoiler and side skirts were new, and the rear quarters were redesigned. There were two filler caps, one on either side, and positioned above the wheelarch. Structurally, the layout of the fuel system had to be changed to install the rear seats, and the pair of tanks normally housed on the Tasmin floor was amalgamated into one 14-gallon tank located above the rear axle.

With the best will in the world, the rear seats of the Tasmin +2 Coupé were really only suitable for carrying young children, whose side vision was in any case impaired by the thick B-pillar. With the front seats fully forward, adults could be carried in the back at a pinch, but the rear glass hatch sloped downwards over the rear seats, making it even more cramped. Also prominent are the inertia-reel seat belt mounting, rear speaker, and useful oddments bin. It was a laudable attempt at producing a TVR for the young family, but disappointingly only forty-seven units were ever made. In 1981 this model cost £14,903.99 including taxes, while the power steering option would have added a further £311.45, with automatic transmission priced at £498.33.

(Opposite, bottom): the +2 coupé body was pressed into service as the basis for the Series 2 Tasmin, while reverting to the twin fuel tank arrangement – note that the filler cap is ahead of the wheelarch – and instead of rear seats there was now a flat luggage platform. This was accessed via the hinged glass hatch, supported on a pair of gas struts, and provided 16 cu-ft of space. The spare wheel is just visible through the glazed rear panel, which provided useful visibility when reversing. The Tasmin S2 Coupé was made between April 1981 and 1985, and 136 units were produced.

The Tasmin was always a distinctive and high profile vehicle, and the factory press car features here as transport in a carnival procession for local starlet 'Miss Fleetwood'. In 1983 the 'Tasmin' name was dropped and the Convertible and the S2 Coupé were renamed the 280i Convertible and 280i Coupé, in line with the company's next step in the progression to more powerful cars – the 350i.

This 280i Coupé was owned by Martin Lilley for some years after his tenure of the company ceased. He has continued to be involved on the periphery, however, often being present at significant TVR Car Club events.

One of the most enduring TVR racers is Colin Blower, who drives a Tuscan in the current Challenge series. Having switched from racing a 3000M in the 1970s, Colin was an early protagonist with the new model. Here he is drifting the Tasmin Convertible round the Mallory Park hairpin in April 1981.

The first really new model produced under Peter Wheeler's ownership of TVR was the 350i, introduced in 1983, but it was externally at least just a facelift of the S1 Tasmin. Here, a Rover V8 engine and gearbox are being installed in a Tasmin chassis. The two SU carbs were later replaced by Lucas fuel injection. Yorkshireman Peter Wheeler is now aged 53. His background was in chemical and pharmaceutical engineering, and he made a successful business of supplying the booming North Sea oil industry with processing equipment and water injection during the 1970s. He was a committed TVR fan, having owned a Taimar Turbo and an early Tasmin, and by the time he took over the reins from Martin Lilley he was already a major shareholder in the company. Wheeler's philosophy has always been to create new models on a regular basis to sustain customer interest.

Typical paddock shot of Colin Blower posing with his 2.8-litre Tasmin during the 1985 Prodsports Championship. Starting from the second row at an Oulton Park round, his opposition consists of Morgan Plus 8s, a Porsche 911SC, a Caterham and numerous Midgets and a Fiat X1/9. One of the Morgan drivers has evidently 'surrendered' without turning a wheel.

A tight fit in an engine compartment originally designed around a Ford V6, the lightweight all-aluminium 3528cc Rover V8 with its Lucas fuel injection was a significant step for TVR. With the 2.8-litre Ford V6 unit approaching the limit of its development potential – and with the engine's distant US parentage making it unsaleable in certain Middle Eastern markets – the British (Buick-derived) engine was the way to go. It produced 190bhp at 5280rpm and 220lb/ft torque at 4000rpm, and was available with Rover five-speed all synchromesh gearbox or General Motors automatic box.

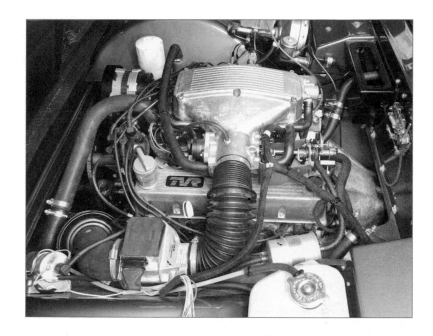

In 1981 TVR came up with a Tasmin Convertible powered by a turbocharged version of the Ford V6 engine. It was a similar installation to that which had already been used in the 3.0-litre units of the M-series Turbos, but the new version was developed by TVR itself. No further progress was made with the Convertible model, but instead they went ahead and made a stunning turbo version of the Tasmin S2 Coupé, shown on the stand at the NEC in October 1982. The bodywork was revised to produce even sharper facets on the corners of the front air-dam and side skirts, and there were Turbo graphics on the window of the glazed rear panel.

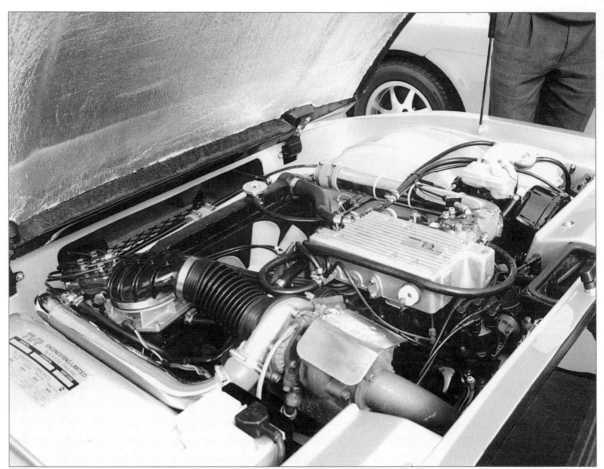

The turbocharged 2.9-litre Ford V6 produced 228bhp and could power the prototype Tasmin Coupé up to 150mph. Had the car gone into production, the price would have been £16,800. It was perhaps not as neat an installation as that of the M-series Turbos, although all the constituent parts were visible and thus more accessible. In the foreground is the turbine with heat shield, and the piping that feeds back to the induction system can be traced running around the front of the engine bay ahead of the radiator. The car is now road registered UKN 692, and is pictured at Blackpool during the TVR Car Club's 'Back Home' meeting.

Production of Tasmin Convertible bodyshells in progress at Bristol Avenue on 2 June 1986. Two shells were made per day, cured overnight and removed from their moulds the next morning. Manufacture was carried out by 23 men, 13 of whom made the actual shells, while the remaining 12 trimmed and finished the shells prior to painting. One task was to remove the temporary windscreen support. The formula for Tasmin shells was 4.5 ounces of fibreglass matting, with reinforcements laid into the moulds in crucial areas to provide better impact resistance and panel rigidity. The laminate was between ⅜in and ⅜₆in (6mm to 10mm), and there was a double thickness of bodywork around the engine bay. The screen and cant rails were boxed using closed-cell foam sections, while the Convertibles were reinforced with steel tubes. Once the fresh shells had emerged from the moulds they were trundled around on slave chassis while work progresses on them. Excess fibreglass was trimmed off, bonnet and boot and doors with side impact beams were fitted, and the body unit was cured for half an hour at 54 degrees centigrade beneath the infra-red mobile arch. The object was to relieve air pockets trapped in the laminates by bringing them to the surface, and further imperfections were attended to manually after baking.

In 1986 the Tasmin 280i Convertible styling was revised to create a Series 3 version. Prominent were the integrated front air-dam that housed new light units and impact absorbing bumpers, and the side skirts moulded into the bodywork. Door mirrors are much more streamlined and better integrated into the styling. There was a revised bonnet design, and the boot spoiler and BBS-type spider's web pattern alloy wheels were standard issue in the retail price of £17,840. By 1986 the 280i was the only model available with automatic transmission.

This 280i pictured with the factory's 420SEAC race car transporter as a backdrop is a 1986 American-spec Series 2 model. The rear spoiler was absent, but the air scoops in the bonnet were common to the 350i model. The 'federalised' model Tasmin and 280i Convertible had been available in the US since spring 1983 with 145bhp emission controlled engine and impact absorbing bumpers.

Interior of the 350i cockpit is typical of the wedge era, with an emphasis on rectangular shapes and straight lines that suit the car's styling very well, apart, perhaps, from the box-like console housing the centrally mounted stereo/heater control panel. TVR's idiosyncratic handbrake location continues to be to the right of the gear lever, while the Momo-style steering wheel lends a touch of class, and similarly, the VDO dials are laid out symmetrically in the walnut veneered instrument panel.

Head-on shot of the 350i, taken by the factory just after the model first came out in 1983. While not so different from the S1 Tasmin, the stance of the 350i is much bolder; growing closer to the macho image that was originally envisaged for the model. Colour coded bumpers and a more dramatic front air dam are partly responsible for the transformation; while integrated driving lights blend in well with the design. Styling of the TVR logo, although bolder, remains much the same as it did in Martin Lilley's day, and the 350i identification appears in a similar font on the splitter of the air-dam. Early cars were badged as Tasmins as well.

TVR Car Club members get to the most charming locations. This is Chris Wright's pristine 350i at Lanercost Priory near Brampton, Cumbria, in 1994. The author has less fond memories of the place, remembering that he was once frog-marched out of a neighbouring farmyard by an irate farmer, while clutching his screaming baby daughter, when all he wanted to do was to get her a drink from his car that was parked at the end of the farm track. Perhaps it was the Border Reivers' sticker that upset him. Anyway, we trust Chris encountered no such hostility on his visit!

This is a later 350i, showing how the car had evolved with a smoother façade by 1985. The front air dam had become more angular and the splitter was now flatter, with the driving lamps slightly recessed. The horizontal flutings across the bumper front were gone and the bonnet was reprofiled. It was now starting to look less extreme, yet there was no mistaking the purposeful chunkiness. The chassis of the 350i was significantly different to that of the Tasmin, as it had been widened by 1.5in around the engine bay. The Tasmin's front suspension had been criticised for being too soft, and the old complaint of steering kickback on undulating road surfaces that had been so familiar in the early 1960s was heard once more. So on the instructions of the company's new chief development director John Box the 350i's front end was altered, with modifications centring on stiffer spring rates and the use of a relocated forward-facing tie bar operating in tension with a fatter anti-roll bar.

Viewed in profile, the lines of the 350i Coupé are all about co-ordinated wedge shapes. Apart from the overall form of the car, which tapers away from the roof in both directions, the front splitter is distinctly wedge-like, as is the one at the trailing edge of the rear skirt. The rear three-quarter shot of Chris Wright's car shows the single petrol filler cap below the B-post, the rear glass panel, BBS-type wheels and the attractive kink of the front wheelarch. Despite its recent origins, the 350i Coupé is far less gawky than the Tasmin model it was sourced from.

Ian Blore's 350i has later styling cues of the 1985 model, including the two tail pipes that emerge from the rear skirt instead of the single exhaust pipe that exited on the left-hand side of the rear skirt on the 1983 model. Paradoxically, there were also late-model cars that had twin tailpipes protruding from the right-hand side of the rear skirt. The 1985 model also has the larger rear light clusters that were sourced from the Renault Fuego coupé, which replaced the more compact Rover saloon rear lights of the earlier cars. By 1987 the 350i had sprouted an aerofoil on its bootlid. The luggage space in these models was never brilliant, with room in the boot for a couple of holdalls and not much else. It would have made a significant difference if the spare wheel had been a space-saver, and of course stowing the central panel of the hood meant another incursion into the carrying capacity. But there again, you can't have everything, and the 350i was exhilarating top-down motoring. Total production of the 350i Convertible between 1983 and 1990 was 872 units.

With this model, TVR took the evolution of the soft-top concept a stage further by fitting a rigid central panel as the cockpit roof, so that there were up to four permutations for open-top motoring. The rear canopy was in fabric, its header linked to the fibreglass roof panel by the rear rollover hoop that could be folded back down if required. Meanwhile, the top was tucked away in the boot. The only downside was that the rear window crazed with age – as they all do – and a zip-out version might have been an advantage.

One variation on the theme was the super-charged SX350, prepared by former Barrow-in-Furness TVR dealer David Haughin. Eleven TVR wedges received the 'blower' treatment, including nine 350is and two 400is. Some cars had 390i shells and SEAC cockpit interiors, and this one is a 1989 SX350 belonging to Jasper Gilder. Supercharging was virtually the norm in pre- and post-war motor racing, but applying it to the Rover V8 was the idea of drag-racing star Dennis Priddle, who advised Haughin on the methodology. The first TVR to receive the treatment was a Sprintex-supercharged 350i – registration E319 EEO – in 1987. To cope with the extra power an uprated suspension package was evolved for all SX conversions, consisting of 420i driveshafts, four-pot calliper front brakes and racing pads, Koni dampers with harder settings and higher spring rates.

As if 3.5-litres doesn't provide you with enough power to play around with! Using the Sprintex S102 supercharger to force more juice into the V8's gaping maw, the SX350 performance was lifted to 270bhp at 5500rpm, giving it a top speed of 150mph and 0–60mph acceleration of 6.3 seconds. It also had the effect of making the engine even more tractable. The supercharger spins at 15,000rpm and can push in air at 500 cu-ft per minute, translating as 75bhp at the flywheel. The car's progress – stinkingly rapid – was accompanied by an extraordinary noise as the high-pitched whine of the supercharger fought for aural supremacy with the bellowing V8. Modifications to the engine were minimal: just thicker head gaskets fitted to lower the compression ratio, and the injection's ECU modified.

The 390SE was introduced in 1984 when TVR raised the capacity of the 3.5-litre V8 engine to 3.9 litres. The conversion was based on enlarging the bores, and was carried out by well-known touring car racer and performance tuning specialist Andy Rouse. Power output was 275bhp, giving a top speed of 150mph and 0–60mph time of 5 seconds. It was the start of an inexorable trend that would eventually take the all-alloy Rover unit up to 5.0 litres, and it also took the company further up-market and into the rarefied 150mph supercar bracket previously accessible only to models running with forced induction. Between 1984 and 1988 they made 103 units of the 390SE, and later on a number of these were fitted with the 4.2-litre engine and badged as 420SEs. The 390SE Series 2 model featured here was first shown at the Northern Motor Show in Manchester in 1986, and its front air-dam was further revised to produce a more shark-like arrangement. The air intake was also protected by a slatted grille. It was carried on into the line of the wheelarches and the side skirts to produce spats and a lip over the arches. At the rear end, the lower valance took the form of a full-width aerofoil, while the door mirrors were faired in and the bonnet now featured a set of louvres on opposite sides near its top and bottom edges. The whole dramatic ensemble was set off by OZ racing wheels shod with fat 225/60 x 15 Yokohama rubber.

Here's a highly polished engine, and this time it's bored out to a full 4.0 litres for the 400SE model.

This is one monster catch; it's a 400SE, belonging to the TVR Car Club's West Sussex regional organiser Jack Acres, pictured on the quayside at St Vaast-la-Hougue on the Cotentin peninsula in Normandy during a French trip in 1997. The 400SE's 3943cc V8 drives through a five-speed gearbox and will pull effortlessly from a standstill, taking off like a rocket over 2500rpm.

The front end of the 400SE was tidied up a little bit more, with the front bumper retracted a little bit and the apron revised slightly to produce a flatter façade, while an additional chin spoiler is evident underneath. On the bootlid is an elevated aerofoil, with the lower valance taking the form of an inverted spoiler designed to glue the car to the road. This is Jack Acres' car at the Goodwood racecourse in 1996 during a club track day – the entire circuit was renovated in 1998. TVR produced 242 examples of the 400SE between 1988 and 1991, and thirty-seven units of the 450SE were made in 1989 and 1990.

By 1986 TVR had become very serious about developing the wedge to its optimum potential, and they produced the 4.2-litre 420 SEAC. The acronym stood for Special Equipment Aramid Composite, which was another way of saying that it had a very special bodyshell, made out of Kevlar, resin and carbon fibre with honeycomb reinforcement in the nose. This is an extraordinarily resilient composite medium, strong yet pliable, and equally important, it is extremely light even compared with fibreglass. It is also very much more expensive than fibreglass, and there is an element of controversy about exactly how many SEACs were made with the Kevlar body and how many were made with identical fibreglass shells. Whatever, the 420 SEAC was built to special order only, and just thirty-seven were made between 1986 and 1988, with a further twenty-eight units of the yet more powerful 450 SEAC made in 1988 and 1989. Each one took between two and three weeks to build – that's some 600 man-hours per car, and in 1989 a 420 SEAC would have cost £31,000.

A 420 SEAC belonging to Sean Hayes receives a once-over at the hands of the scrutineers in the Silverstone pits garage during a TVR Car Club National Track Day, 25 August 1996. Before any car is allowed to take to the track on these occasions, the authorities need to be satisfied that nothing is loose, leaking or about to drop off. Even rear light clusters are suitably taped over. The stands may be empty, but such occasions allow enthusiast owners to explore the outer limits of their car's potential without too much fear of embarrassment.

Outwardly, the 420 SEAC may be endowed with the most extreme appearance of all the TVR wedge models, but on the other hand its interior is undoubtedly the most civilised. The instruments are discreet, legible and neatly housed in the walnut dash, while the central console display is altogether better integrated into the dashboard and transmission tunnel. Its leather upholstery gives the cockpit a sumptuous air, set off by the smart Momo steering wheel. By no means did all SEACs have power steering, because of the model's competition derivation, but without it parking would not be easy because of its wide Bridgestone RE71 tyres.

During 1986 and 1987 the works racing 420 SEAC was developed by Chris Schirle and driven by Steve Cole, and it trounced everything that came its way. That is, until it got banned by the authorities on the grounds of not being a genuine production sports car. Which was not the case; TVR could, and does, produce more or less anything it feels like. It won nineteen out of twenty-four races in the 750 Motor Club's production sportscar series, and was class winner in the BARC sports-saloon challenge. In 1987 it led around the daunting street circuit of the Macau Grand Prix, with Steve Cole building up a full minute's lead in the wet; eventually he was narrowly beaten by John Kent in the 3.0-litre Cosworth-powered TVR S. The 420 SEAC race car was pensioned off, and bought, via DG Racing and Hong Kong, by its current owner Jeff Statham in 1991. It was expertly restored by him and repainted by Jim Gamsby during the next three years, and appears much as it did in the late '80s, seen here at Brands Hatch during a TVR Car Club Track Day in the hands of Jeff Statham. Racing improves the breed, as they say, and the results of the factory's successes on the track were swiftly applied to the other production models. Best example of this was the implementation of a new independent rear suspension layout, consisting of lower wishbones and radius arms.

At the heart of the 420 SEAC race car is the thundering 350bhp 4,228cc Rover V8, surmounted by four Dell'Orto 48 carburettors and ITG air filters. The Tuscan-spec engine was last rebuilt by Graham Nash of TVR Power in Coventry, and has Aeroquip fuel and oil lines, plus silicon water hoses fitted, and internally there is an octet of 12:1 high-compression Cosworth pistons. It has a cross-bolt block, implying that sixteen bolts instead of the normal eight secure the crankshaft. This unique car has high-lift camshafts and Group A rocker gear (derived from the TWR Rover SD1 touring cars) consisting of special large-diameter shafts with Volvo offset rockers, with polished and ported heads. Its competition spec includes dry-sump lubrication and special manifolding

that produces an additional 85bhp. All this power was deployed through a Getrag racing gearbox with a direct fifth ratio and a Salisbury limited slip differential. This has the added sophistication of its own propshaft-driven oil pump and cooler.

Using the 3.9-litre Rover V8 engine, the Speed Eight prototype was a possible successor to the wedge cars, and was displayed at the 1989 Motor Show. Clearly, its proportions were similar to its predecessors', but the corners had been rounded off and, arguably, its lines now hinted at the Ferrari 365 GTS/4 Daytona convertible. It was already evident that the design was pointing towards the Griffith, and it was no coincidence that the rotund Tuscan race cars were launched the same year. Peter Wheeler had always admired the look of macho 1950s sports cars, and it was natural that his vision for TVR's future styling would veer to the retrospective. The Speed Eight was built as a 2 + 2 with the intention that small children could be carried in the well behind the seats, and had it gone into production, would have been TVR's first convertible 2 + 2. The leather-padded and walnut-veneered dashboard also included the type of adventurous moulding that accompanied the Griffith.

Known as the 'White Elephant', this beast was a prototype made especially for Peter Wheeler in 1988, and powered by a 5.0-litre Holden V8 engine coupled to a Borg Warner T5 gearbox. There was a possibility at the time of a deal with General Motors for TVR to use Holden engines – which had an advanced engine management system – and a Holden engineer was even sent over from Australia to assist with setting the car up. The White Elephant was built on a 390i chassis, modified to accommodate the larger iron-block engine, with a 390 body altered internally to provide a third seat for Peter Wheeler's dog. Externally, the 390 shell was covered in a layer of moulding foam and fibreglassed over, and a Tasmin Coupé roof and rear screen were bonded in place. The screen came from an earlier prototype, the 1986 420 Sports Saloon, which was a rather angular 2 + 2 design. The White Elephant's bonnet was in Kevlar and the frontal lighting arrangement was to Peter Wheeler's own specification. Apart from the unusual engine, the White Elephant had a proper lower wishbone front suspension and was used as a factory hack for some time, until it landed awkwardly after taking a hump-back bridge at speed. This caused the engineers to reconsider the routing of TVR exhaust pipes, which had previously exited below the chassis, and the arrangement would be different on the Griffith. The White Elephant was a fairly logical progression of the Tasmin Coupé shape, and perhaps what it ought to have looked like in the first place. In 1998 the car was stored at Birmingham TVR dealers Team Central, and was used by proprietor Clive Greenhalgh as a show car on high days and holidays.

CHAPTER FOUR

MODERN TIMES

A self-confessed fan of classic sportscar styling from the 1950s, coupled with big engine performance, Peter Wheeler soon made sure that TVR's state-of-the-art designs reflected these two criteria. By the 1990s it seemed he could do no wrong.

Seen from behind, the Tuscan Speed Six's posterior is still the roundest rump in the business. Only now, the tail-light cluster is quite different from the original Griffith model, set high in the upper corner of the wing rather than at waist height. The stop, rear, and indicator lenses peer out from cute little caves apparently sculpted out of the bodyshell and covered in a perspex fairing that goes some way to matching the ones at the front. The Tuscan Speed Six chassis is all new, and 3in longer than the Griffith's. The suspension system remains much as before, with concave profile seven-spoke 7.5in x 16in alloy wheels and Cerbera-spec brakes.

This is the TVR S, which heralded a return to the rounded shapes that, prior to the Tasmin, the company had always been noted for. It was a significant move because it reminded the sportscar-buying public that TVRs didn't have to be wedge-shaped, and significantly it was £2,000 cheaper than the out-going 280i that had been the contemporary entry level model. Unveiled at the National Exhibition Centre in 1986, the S's stylistic connections with the late '70s M-series 3000S were obvious. Its timing was impeccable, coinciding with a burgeoning interest in classic cars.

These Dutch TVRs are on a tour of Germany, with Anholt Castle in the background. They serve to illustrate the differences between the frontal aspects of the 1970s 3000M, left, and the S2 of 1989. The older car has characteristic embossed moulding on the bonnet, while the later model has a prominent air scoop. In fact there were no components in common between the two. The S was longer and wider, the styling was subtly different around the lights and the rear end, it had wind-up windows and no scoop to the door top, and like the 350i, the rear soft top and support hoop could be kept raised and the car driven in Targa-top form. The TVR S chassis had fewer square-section tubes than the old M-chassis had, and there were now independent wishbones, anti-roll bar, coil springs and dampers up front, and wishbones, semi-trailing arms, coil springs and dampers at the rear.

Trying hard in his S2 is Chris Wright, arm-twirling during a TVR Car Club Track Day in 1995 at Cadwell Park, Britain's mini-Nürburgring. There could be a certain amount of scuttle shake when driven hard, although the S2 was ergonomically well thought out: the left elbow slotted into the little well on the transmission tunnel, and the arm-rest on the door supported the right knee and thigh (in a right-hand-drive car.) The TVR S was greeted with such a positive reception that Peter Wheeler was moved to consider other retrospective designs, which were to materialise subsequently in the Tuscan, Griffith and Chimaera. As the S was developed, the original model became known as the S1 as its successor, the S2, was announced in 1989. The S2 model had the benefit of the slightly larger capacity 2.9-litre Ford Cologne V6 engine with three-way catalytic converter, which enabled it to achieve 135mph and get from 0 to 60mph in 7 seconds. The principal upgrading of the S1's appearance into the S2 was the tidy incorporation of driving lamps into the front valance, while the S2 and subsequent S models ran on attractive eight-pointed star pattern alloy wheels shod with 205/60VR x 15 Bridgestone tyres.

This is a 1991 S3, and the main difference can be seen in the length of the door, which is 5in longer in the S3 than the S2. Clearly this makes for easier access into and out of the car. Differences in the cockpit centred on the instrumentation, which in the earlier model consisted of minor gauges and warning lights set out in an arc in the centre console just to the driver's left, while in the S3 there was a horizontal, split level arrangement. The contours were just starting to veer towards the wraparound look that would become a recognised TVR feature. Seats could be trimmed in a mixture of cloth and vinyl, with half and full leather upholstery optional. There was a four-spoke leather-rim wheel, and for wood lovers, an extravagant full walnut veneer dashboard and console if required. The S3 continued to use the cast-iron 2933cc Ford V6 power unit with its Bosch K-Jetronic fuel injection.

This is a 1991 S3, belonging to Dave Farrell, and photographed in July 1997 at the Royal Naval Air Station at Yeovilton, with 899 Naval Air Squadron's Sea Harrier trained behind. The S3 continued to use the cast-iron 2933cc Ford V6 power unit.

Here is a V8S being a bit of a handful in the wet at the TVR Car Club's East Midlands Track Day at Curborough in May 1997. The V8 model was developed from a works prototype known as the ES back in the late '80s, on which all the obvious vices were tamed, and was introduced in 1991. The engine was TVR's regular 3950cc Rover V8, built by its Coventry-based subsidiary TVR Power who sourced the engines direct from Land Rover at Solihull. Maximum power was 240bhp at 5250rpm, with maximum torque of 270lb/ft at 3000rpm.

Another Track Day, and this time it's Goodwood in February 1996, with a V8S powering away from other club members with a couple of Griffiths and a Grantura waiting their turn. The visual hallmark of the V8S was the large hump on the right rear of the bonnet needed to enclose the 3.9-litre Rover/TVR Power engine. The performance figures for this model give it a top speed of 148mph, with a 0–60mph time of 4.9 seconds, which is pretty rapid by any standards.

The S3 model was produced between 1990 and 1992, when 112 units were made. The later cars were designated S3C, and can be distinguished from the S3 by their smooth bonnet that has no air scoop. Most abundant of the S models was the S2, of which they made 1,443, and there were 605 examples manufactured of the original S1. TVR has never released a figure for the S4, which lasted from 1992 to 1994. The SV8 was in production between 1991 and 1994, and again, the company remains silent on quantities produced. The reputation of the S models is that the newer the car, the better made it would be.

Another example of the TVR public relations department's excellent publicity photography: here is the V8S press car in a picturesque setting, showing off its driving lamps. Since virtually every new TVR has been made to a customer's specific requirements, there can be some extraordinary combinations of paint finish and trim. This vehicle had rather more conventional red coachwork and pale grey leather interior.

The interior of the V8S shows the main dials set in a walnut panel and shrouded by a single binnacle behind the steering column, with auxiliary clocks angled towards the driver over the centre console. Radio/cassette player and heater controls are housed here, while gaitered gear lever and handbrake fit snugly on and alongside the typically high and wide transmission tunnel. Door linings and seats are ergonomically well shaped, and upholstered in pale grey leather with contrasting red piping.

The forward-hinged bonnet makes for easy access to the 3.9-litre Rover/TVR Power engine of the V8S. In the foreground are the plates giving the build data including VIN number, engine number and body code, vehicle type approval number, gross weight, and front and rear axle weights. The all-alloy engine is topped by the plenum chamber serving its electronic fuel injection, while the forward routing of the V8's manifolding can also be seen. A number of SV8s had their engines sleeved down to just under 2.0 litres especially for the Italian market, to get them under the crucial 2-litre tax break. Any deficit in performance was more than compensated for by the addition of a supercharger.

This V8S belonging to Chris Weaver has something of a celebrated pedigree. It was class winner three years running in the concours competition at the TVR Car Club's Back Home event from 1994 to 1996, and second overall in the same event in 1997; and also class winner at TVR Mania, Nottingham, in 1996 as well as Golden Mania at Brands Hatch in 1997. In addition to this, it is also given an airing in a variety of sprints, hillclimbs and track days, such as the Midland Speed Championship round at Curborough.

This is TVR's engine development supremo John Ravenscroft giving the prototype Griffith a motorway shakedown. This car was first seen at the 1990 Birmingham Motor Show, having evolved from the 1988 white Tuscan prototype show car. The obvious difference from the production models is that it has exterior door handles instead of the revolutionary system of buttons and balls.

TVR revived another name from its past when the new Griffith was launched at the 1991 Motor Show, where it was displayed with the OZ split-rim latticework alloy wheels. Its pure, curving body contours came as such a breath of fresh air to the world of sports car motoring, which lavished it with plaudits, to the extent that TVR's reputation promptly improved in leaps and bounds with each successive rave review. Here was a car that captured the moment, arriving on public view at the right time with the right specification.

More readily associated with Griffiths of a different generation, Martin Lilley drove a current model in the 1990s, carrying his own number plate MAL 3. The car's rotund rear quarters are set off by the wide alloy wheels — 7in x 15 at the front and 7.5in x 16 at the rear. Power steering is optional, and allows a wider front tyre to be used. Without power assistance, front tyres are 205/55 x 15, or 225/50 x 15 with assistance, while 245/45 x 16 remains constant at the rear.

The Griffith shares the same foolproof wet-weather gear as the S-range — including the detachable carbon-fibre central roof panel and fold-down rear header, all hand-trimmed in mohair fabric. But getting it off the line here at RAF Benson in 1997 will need some careful control of the foot pedals to avoid embarrassing wheelspin. Naturally, the Griffith has a limited slip diff, which helps get the power down. The chassis and wishbone suspension of the Griffith had been honed on the circuit in the 420 SEAC and Tuscan racing cars, and it was certainly capable of transmitting all that power to the road. To make it a little less uncompromising on undulating B-roads and country lanes as well as potholed city streets, the suspension's Bilstein gas-dampers, anti-roll bars and spring rates were softened up slightly, although there was no compromise on the Griffith's braking potential. It was equipped with big ventilated discs all round to dissipate the heat, while power assisted steering was a sound option for city drivers. The towering specification of the Griffith was by no means unprecedented, but coupled with its pure lines, it redefined the archetypal front engined sportscar, harking back to the Aston Martin DBRs, Ferrari 735LMs and Maserati 150S sports racing cars of the mid-1950s. These were Peter Wheeler's formative years of course, and the Griffith captured the mood of the same generation as well as those who had become interested in the classic car movement more recently. In marketing terms, the strategy of introducing such a beautifully elegant car was excellent, although there is a feeling that Wheeler operates on a more altruistic plane than that.

(Opposite, bottom): the cockpit of a 4.0-litre 1993 Griffith is a beguiling environment, its centrepiece being that delightful elliptical wooden instrument panel topped by the curving leather-clad dash and scuttle top. The whole ensemble is beautifully integrated, and includes a Pioneer stereo system, panel of warning lights, and no extraneous dials. The gear knob is in aluminium with the handbrake to its left in the dished recess in the traditional central console. The seats are individually tailored, and can recline as well as having built-in head restraints. The full-hide treatment is optional.

Who said the Griffith wasn't a family car? This owner on the Promenade at Blackpool for the Back Home meeting shows how you can carry a small child by strapping a child seat into the passenger seat. But the problems arise when the child's other parent wants to come too.

The all-alloy TVR Power/Rover V8 lump is a perfect fit in the Griffith's engine bay, with its rear-hinged bonnet. No matter how many of these power units one sees, the girth of the exhaust manifold trunking is always breathtaking. As you'd expect, catalytic converters and fuel injection are fitted, and the water-cooled eight-cylinder engine has 16 valves. The radiator is set low behind the air intake with cooling fan almost horizontal. Compression ratio is 9.8:1. The power output of the 3,950cc version is 240bhp at 5250rpm, with maximum torque of 270lb/ft at 4000rpm. Top speed is 152mph, with 0–60mph accomplished in 4.7 seconds.

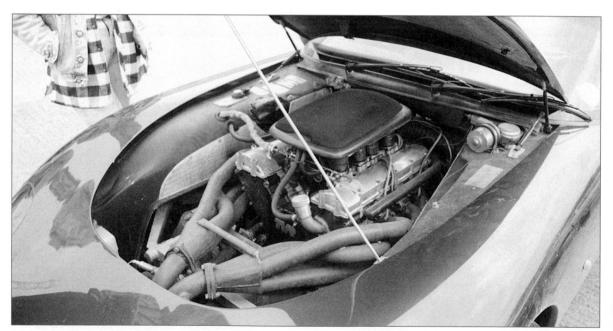

Peter Wheeler was not content to rely on the long-lived and unburstable Rover V8 power unit, and in the early 1990s he took the bold step of building TVR's own engine. This was known as the AJP engine – named after the first initials of Al Melling, who conceived the idea of a modular engine, John Ravenscroft, TVR's engine supremo, and Peter Wheeler himself. Starting from a clean sheet, the AJP engine was constructed in-house, and its modular construction meant it could be produced as a V6, V8, V12 or an in-line configuration. This under-bonnet shot of a Griffith is very unusual, in that the motor is an experimental AJP V8 engine, fitted in November 1994. The TVR casting can be seen just below the V of the cylinder heads.

The boot of the Griffith and Tuscan Speed Six provides a reasonable amount of luggage space, and it is lined throughout in carpet. The fuel tank is clad in insulation material. Capacity becomes somewhat restricted when the carbon-fibre lid of the Targa top is stowed away, however. The boot lid is rear-hinged and supported on a pair of gas struts. There is an electronic boot release that does away with the need for external buttons. Griffiths have remote central locking, as well as stereo radio/cassette player with twin door speakers as standard.

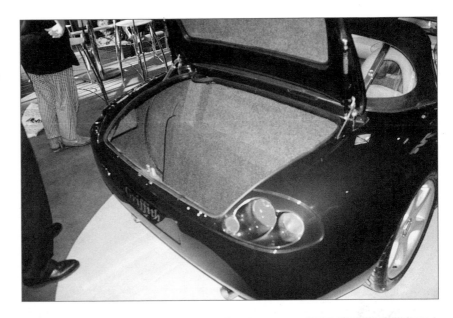

In 1993 the intention at TVR was that production of the regular Griffith would be temporarily suspended in order to get the AJP engine into production, and in order to utilise the Griffith's powertrain and mechanicals the Chimaera was launched. However, such was the demand for the Griffith that the 500 model was introduced, ostensibly as a stop gap until it could receive the AJP engine. A small company like TVR can respond quickly to such demands, and the 90-degree TVR Power/Rover V8 was bored out to a full 5.0 litres — or 4988cc to be precise. Power output rose to 350bhp and maximum torque to 350lb/ft, and there were now only a very few supercars that could live with the Griffith 500.

Driver's eye view of the Griffith 500 dashboard, which is typically elegant and well appointed. The scuttle top and console are clad in leather, with a contrasting walnut veneer for the instrument panel. The heating and ventilation controls were redesigned from the original Griffith, while the cluster of console-mounted golf-ball doorknobs was a brilliant innovation. The competition-derived leather-rim Personal steering wheel adds to the aura of quality.

The Chimaera was launched at the Birmingham NEC in 1992. A true beast in terms of performance and stature, its nomenclature followed on conveniently behind the Griffith, itself a name redolent of the mythological Griffin, despite its origins back in the '60s as the surname of a US car dealer. The Chimaera went all the way into bestiality, being named after a legendary fire-breathing creature with a lion's head, a goat's body and the tail of a dragon, which apparently spent its time devastating the Middle East – until it was slain.

The wraparound dashboard and scuttle topography of the Chimaera is not so different from that of the Griffith, although there is different grouping of the minor dials. They have yellow faces with black numbers, forming a strong contrast with the dark brown walnut of the instrument panel. The Chimaera cockpit is just as inviting as its sibling's, and the moulding of the interior panels neatly reflects the meaty, bulbous shape of the car's exterior. Standard interior equipment includes electric windows, tinted glass, radio/cassette player, central locking, Personal leather-rim wheel, an adjustable pedal box, leather seat facings, an ice detector, and a microwave alarm system.

This is a Tim Andrew shot, taken in 1993 while Tipler was involved in a back-to-back road test for the late lamented *Car Week* magazine, between a 4.3-litre Chimaera and an MGB R-V8. The TVR proved fantastically tractable over a mixture of fast Cotswolds A-roads and back lanes, and its interior stayed snug and dry in the rain while the Rover product's most certainly did not. In terms of ride and handling there was no contest, and the TVR felt absolutely in a class of its own. On back roads, the steering reports every nuance of the road surface, loading up strongly as lock is applied. It is at its best on swooping, dipping and diving roads, where it feels superbly balanced and responds to everything asked of it.

While the Griffith was a sleek, elongated egg shape with as few intrusions as possible into flowing lines, the Chimaera was another matter. While there was no denying the appeal of its rounded wings, nose and sill panels, there was a different expression about them. They were composed to be provocative, adding up to a coherent design that was far more pugilistic and extrovert in its effect. So what you get is a more aggressive looking car, and because of these idiosyncrasies of design I believe it is a car that you could live with for longer than the Griffith, because there would always be a fascination with its intricacies.

The Chimaera's frontal aspect is full of drama, with beautifully sculpted air intakes, lights and indicator niches catching the eye, vying for prominence with the slashes down the sides of the bonnet. An absence of bumpers always enhances a purposeful appearance, and TVRs have this in abundance. This 450 model belongs to Andy Hutcheson, and the hangar-like building behind it is equally dramatic: it's the American Air Museum at Duxford Air Museum, designed by Sir Norman Foster and opened in 1997.

If the Griffith shape is reminiscent of certain svelte mid-'50s exotica, then the Chimaera, viewed in profile here at Duxford, has more of the brutish appeal of the Lister Jaguar, Ferrari TR250, or Maserati 350S of broadly similar vintage. Like its sister car, the Chimaera also has the styling feature where the door's leading edge appears to fold away under the trailing edge of the front wing. Travelling in the Targa top format pictured here, with the roof's centre panel removed, the occupants have the best of both worlds – a blast of fresh air with no buffeting whatsoever from the wind.

Short of a full-race Tuscan, there's little to match the sound and the fury of a 4.0-litre Chimaera V8 on full song, and it really does signify something: 235bhp produced at 5500rpm, or 260lb/ft of torque at 4500rpm, accompanied by the most glorious sound track, redolent of CanAm or TransAm racers. The Chimaera was also available with 4.3- and 5.0-litre versions of the TVR Power/Rover V8 unit. The windscreen wipers, top left, provide a source for the washer jets, located at the top corner of the wiper arms.

In the hot seat here is Len Messenger, hard at work in his Chimaera at the wonderfully undulating Brands Hatch circuit on a TVR Car Club Track Day. The car remains poised owing to its typical TVR-spec multi-tubular backbone chassis and independent wishbone suspension all round. Gas dampers and coil springs, plus anti-roll bars, are fitted front and back. It is hauled up by servo-assisted dual-circuit 240mm ventilated discs at the front and 250mm discs at the rear. Prodigious grip is provided by 205/60ZR x 15 and 225/55ZR x 16 Bridgestone RE71 tyres.

Here is the Chimaera in its element, rushing up to the Druids Hairpin at Brands Hatch having plunged down that stomach-churning descent of Paddock Hill bend, into the dip at the bottom, then rumbling up Hailwood Hill before driver Len Messenger treads hard on the brakes and sets it all up for the hairpin. There's nothing like a few laps of a race circuit for getting the fullest enjoyment out of your car, because you can (within recognised limits) explore its performance and handling potential more thoroughly than on the public highway, while honing your own driving technique into the bargain. If you lose the car, chances are you'll land in a gravel trap and not bend it either. The downside is that insurance policies tend to fly out of the window.

TVRs have almost always been two seaters, and Peter Wheeler has publicly denounced four-door cars with single occupancy as a waste of space. But one of the questions most frequently asked of him was 'When are you going to make a four-seater?' His reply was to the effect that he would consider it if the market looked as if it would support one. By 1993 the Cerbera was being designed, and the four-seater coupé was once again a reality – if more of a 2 + 2.

Here, a pre-production Cerbera gets the once over from enthusiasts during a TVR Car Club factory visit in 1994. With bonnet removed, the fit of the 4.2-litre AJP8 engine and its attendant mixture of steel, alloy and carbon-fibre trunking can be better appreciated. It features a steel flat-plane crank, with big-end journals at 180 degrees to one another. Because of the harmonics that resulted from eight cylinders in the 75-degree configuration it was necessary to implement an unconventional firing order, which means the AJP unit sparks at 75 and 105 degrees in the crankshaft's rotation. An efficient by-product of the exhaust manifold system allows each cylinder to help exhaust another. In accord with its name, the Cerbera emits a sharp bark, unlike the rumbling Rover-derived V8s of the other models.

The Cerbera was the first TVR coupé to be built since 1989, and the first 2 + 2 since the 280i 2+2 Coupé of 1985. It was built on a new chassis, similar in design to the Griffith and Chimaera, but 6in longer. With TVR model names being sourced from ancient mythology, it was logical to give the new car a similar identity. And bearing in mind the Chairman's penchant for dogs, it was appropriate to call it Cerbera, after Cerberus, the multi-headed, snake-tailed canine supposed to have guarded the entrance to the underworld. Viewed from the rear, the Cerbera has much of the Chimaera's tail about it. It also has a built-in steel frame roll-cage, hidden within the roof pillars of the closed bodywork. The suspension was of a similar layout to the rest of the range, but set up especially for the heavier, longer wheelbase car. Equally significantly, the Cerbera was fitted with the company's own 4.2-litre AJP8 engine: Peter Wheeler was determined to create a British engine for his cars, seeing Rover post-BMW take-over as somehow tainted by its Germanic ownership. This compact 75-degree, lightweight all-aluminium unit, weighing about the same as the legendary Cosworth DFV Formula 1 engine, had a conventional single camshaft per bank and two valves per cylinder design, but an unusual firing order. It developed 350bhp at a relatively high 6500rpm, and 320lb/ft of torque at 4500rpm. Many AJP8 engine components are of extremely high quality, such as the forged pistons and connecting rods and the rifle-bored camshafts that are made of solid billet EN40B steel.

Compared with its siblings, the four-seat Cerbera is quite a long car, at 4280mm, and the chassis design reflects this. Clearly they had to ensure that it did not flex and thereby compromise the integrity of the suspension, and everything had to be uprated to cope with the increased performance of the AJP8 engine as well as the potential additional weight of two extra passengers. This is a factory promotional shot of a 4.5-litre model in a woodland glade: peak power goes up to 420bhp at 6750rpm with maximum torque at 380lb/ft at 5500rpm.

It's a wet August day at RAF Benson in 1997, and in these circumstances most folk like to be warm and dry. There's no reasoning with some people, however, and this Cerbera and its occupants are all set for a blast – probably sideways, as the dog wags its tail, and notwithstanding a limited slip diff or optional Hydratrak traction control system – down the main runway. Still, it is a closed coupé, so at least they're unlikely to get sodden. This magnificent beast can top 160mph, and make 60mph from rest in 4.2 seconds, and in this environment there are no constraints on exercising such stunning performance. But it's wet, so do they dare?

Well, perhaps 180 max is pushing it a bit. It will do over 160 though. This is an interesting view of a Cerbera in the Cadwell Park car park, showing off the elegant curve of the trailing edge of that long, long door and its semi-frameless windows, as well as the forward hinged boot lid lifted up. As befits its bigger chassis, the Cerbera has wider boots than the Chimaera, with 225/45ZR x 16 Bridgestones at the front, and 235/50ZR x 16s at the rear.

'Best of British' may be a cliché, but not in this case as a Cerbera 4.3 meets an RAF Harrier GR3, two of the finest pieces of engineering in their respective fields.

If the interiors and dashboards of the Griffith and Chimaera were refreshingly innovative, that of the Cerbera was something different again. There was even more of the wraparound feel to the cabin, with myriad sinuous curving forms. The main dials – black figures on white clocks – and warning lights are housed in a neat binnacle right ahead of the driver, while the clock and fuel gauge are, surprisingly, found in a separate pod underneath the steering column, between the driver's knees in fact. The handsome two-spoke steering wheel is the home for wiper, horn and headlight dip thumb-tip control buttons, while the stereo and massive speaker occupy the centre console. The gearlever is slightly taller than before and the handbrake lever appears more prominent.

Four seats maybe, but those in the rear of the Cerbera are best occupied by children – unless the adults settle for short journeys and plenty of leg stretching. However, there is more room in the 'Tiv' than a great many other would-be 2 + 2s. The figure hugging, leather-upholstered reclining seats are as comfortable as they look, and the straight-leg driving position requires no compromise. Like the steering wheel, the pedal box is also adjustable enabling the perfect driving position to be found.

The Cerbera specification includes all the usual features present in the other TVRs, but in this case electric window switches and heater controls are in polished aluminium, while air conditioning is optional. The doors have no handles, but release buttons in the door pocket and on the key fob, which also controls the remote alarm and engine immobiliser. In fact, there is no ignition key as such: when the immobiliser has been programmed, the engine is started by the black ignition button beneath the steering wheel, and stopped by the red button to its left.

At the 1997 Earls Court Show TVR unveiled the Tuscan Speed Six. In reality it was the productionised Griffith Speed Six shown at the NEC in 1996, and was presented as a completely new model since the Griffith 500 continued to be available. To create the Tuscan Speed Six, the existing Griff body was altered in a number of ways, including revised headlight nacelles that incorporated the indicators, shark's mouth air intake, and angled louvres in the bonnet.

The Tuscan Speed Six's interior design is surely radical enough for even the most ardent futurist, shielding the driver in an almost pure semi-circular inner cockpit, which serves to frame the instrumentation. Gone is the traditional dashboard, and the key dials are set jewel-like in a cluster on top of the steering column, with fuel gauge and ventilator suspended below it. The now-traditional aluminium 'golf-balls' lodge in a separate leather-covered arm that criss-crosses under the semi-circular arch and curves on over the passenger-side foot-well. And posing on a shelf under the arch is a Pioneer stereo.

Here's what the Tuscan Speed Six is really all about, the classic 4.0-litre straight-six engine. It is a variant of the AJP theme, made possible because of the modular concept of TVR's own power unit. The road-going Tuscan is the first TVR to use a straight-six engine since the 2500M, but the 3996cc Speed Six unit is light years away from the old Triumph lump in terms of neatness and sophistication. It is all-aluminium, canted over at 15 degrees, with chain-driven overhead twin-cam 24-valve head, and dry-sump lubrication that allows it to sit low in the chassis. It has a compression ratio of 11:1, and pumps out 360bhp at 7000rpm, and 320lb/ft of torque at 5250rpm. From 1997 the Speed Six engine was also available in the Cerbera.

If the notorious nude models stole the show for TVR back in 1971, the Speed Twelve prototype did it all on its own at the 1997 Earls Court event. Compared with the vast majority of mundane machinery present, it could have come from another planet. And in a way it did: the planet Blackpool, where they dare to be different. Amazed punters and press were agog. Could this extraordinary device really make it to production as a road car? The answer, as has often been the case as far as Peter Wheeler is concerned, was to wait and see, and to gauge the reaction and level of interest before giving it the green light.

The Speed Twelve prototype was obviously meant to be regarded as a potential racing car, with its fixed Kevlar-shelled race seats, minimalist dashboard, chunky Personal steering wheel – detachable and with ignition kill-switch – and exposed adjustable pedal box. Information is relayed via a combination of analogue and LCD dials, and the tachometer is the single prominent instrument facing the driver, while the speedo is relegated to the ally-look swathe to the left. A roll-cage is not fitted here, although it would be for competition purposes, and should anyone wish to use the Speed Twelve just as a road car, the appropriate level of cosseting could be applied simply.

The car gets its name from its awe-inspiring twelve-cylinder 7.7-litre V12 engine. In unrestricted form, it is capable of a colossal 240mph, and produces 800bhp at 7250rpm and 650lb/ft of torque at 5750rpm. It is a member of the AJP modular range, and features 48-valve aluminium cylinder heads mounted on a high molybdenum EN14T steel block, with EN40B nitrided steel crank and EN24B conrods. The Speed Twelve pushes out 800bhp per tonne, a considerable advance on that other paragon of road-racing, the McLaren F1 (which delivers 550bhp per tonne).

CHAPTER FIVE

THE BRISTOL AVENUE FACTORY

TVRs are entirely built at the factory, and unlike other specialist motor manufacturers the company is becoming increasingly self-sufficient, to the extent that it designs and builds its own AJP range of engines.

A mixture of brand-new TVRs undergoing pre-delivery inspection in the service garage where four ramps are available. Customers can also bring older models for special maintenance work.

TVR Engineering's Bristol Avenue factory is located in Blackpool's northern residential suburb amid 1930s red-brick terraced houses, and the bright lights of the Golden Mile promenade and the seaside Tower are about a mile away. Dating from before the 1971 move, the original plant consisted of a motley collection of single-storey brick and concrete workshops, but in 1995 the company expanded into the much larger two-storey premises – a 1930s laundry – next door. Since then, the final assembly department, trimming, electrical, servicing, quality control and stores have been located here. This 1993 shot shows a couple of bare 350 shells in the central compound, which was where they were stored.

By 1995 the car park compound had been temporarily filled up with half-finished Chimaera shells on slave chassis, while in the background the wedges had found a final resting place on top of a container. The building behind is the Tuscan racing and development shop. During 1996 and 1997 TVR began producing the Chimaera in Malaysia, using the local labour force at a factory at Port Klang near Kuala Lumpur.

While Peter Wheeler has the final say in deciding what shapes should go into prototype stage, the cars are styled by Damian McTaggart (left), and Nick Coughlan. There is some crossover, but generally Damian does the interiors and Nick shapes the exteriors, with additional input from John Ravenscroft. There are very few drawings or 'renderings', and instead the proposed design is built up on an existing buck, which is coated with a thick layer of insulation foam, applied with spatulas. Once hard, it can be cut, sliced, pared and gouged into whatever shape is required, using planes, saws, hammer and chisel, even bread-knives. A fresh coat of foam covers any unwanted details, and in this way the basic ideas for the new shape evolve. Shut-lines and light clusters are marked out in black tape. No other manufacturers design their cars this way, yet TVR is sufficiently flexible that if Wheeler approves an idea it can very quickly be turned into a prototype.

Surely no other car manufacturer can claim to have a dog on its design team. But TVR does: legend has it that Peter Wheeler's amiable German Pointer, Ned, took a bite out of the nose of the prototype Chimaera buck during a boisterous scuffle with stylist Nick Coughlan, and hence the dog's tooth-shaped recesses for the indicators. This energetic canine has the run of the factory, and if you ring up the company the chances are you'll hear Ned sounding off in the background. Or if you visit – or work there – and you leave your sandwiches unattended, Ned'll have them. But they're used to it, so you'll be able to claim from his expense account for replacements.

Before the TVR's chassis tubes can be welded together, they have to be measured and cut to length in the machine shop. No less than 47 yards of mild steel tube are used in the creation of a TVR chassis. The machine shop area has expanded considerably since the new premises were acquired, and spilled out into the spacious workshop that was the old final assembly area. The tubes that form the TVR chassis frame are welded together in perfectly triangulated jigs, and assembled in sections that gradually go together to form the complete chassis. The front sub-section is the first element to be created, followed by the rear portion, and these are then joined to the centre section. Chassis builders work in pairs on either side of the jigs, and are masked up to protect their eyes from the brilliant sparks of the welding torches. The torches are fed their spelter from spools of copper wire. Joints are spot-welded first, then the connection of the tubes is completed by seam-welding around the join. By the mid-1990s they were making four chassis a day. Wishbones are also fabricated in jigs and the pick-up points for these are welded on to the completed chassis, along with engine mounts, gearbox brackets and tow eyes.

The chassis has been powder-coated red, which signifies that it was destined for an S model. Those of the Griffith and Chimaera were powder coated silver. To become self-sufficient at this, TVR bought the powder-coating oven from local coachbuilders Duple and Plaxtons when it closed down in 1990. Because of the length of the body-building process, chassis tend to be made three or four weeks in advance. Here, the chassis is being fitted with its suspension, including wishbones and hubs.

Supported on trestles here is a Chimaera chassis, fitted with wishbones, coil springs and dampers, suspension uprights, anti-roll bar, hubs and brake discs. Brake pipe runs are clipped to the frame with plastic tags. The engine bay presents a wide-open space, while the backbone is comprehensively triangulated. The corners of the outriggers are also thoroughly braced. Completed chassis are dispatched to the body shop to have their shells fitted.

Caught in a rare moment of inactivity — otherwise known as a tea break — a pair of Chimaera chassis are in the process of being fettled side by side, with an S4 chassis at the rear. Normally four men at a time work on a single chassis. On the closest chassis, the rear wishbones are open at their fullest extent waiting for the rest of the suspension componentry. The wishbones of the S models were made in-house, combined with Ford uprights coil-springs and dampers, reverting to a semi-trailing arm set-up at the rear.

TVR moulds are good for about 800 applications, after which time shells start to need more work in finishing. The first stage in laying up a mould is to impregnate the fibreglass matting with resin, and smaller sections like these are then worked into the nooks and crannies of the body mould. Areas that need greater strength will be built up with several layers of matting. Fibreglass is such an irritant that gloves are obviously a necessity and goggles are sometimes worn, although breathing apparatus might not go amiss.

This is the body mould for a Chimaera from the rear end, only it is upside down, in order for the artisan to lay-in the fibreglass matting and gel mix. Handfuls of tiny glassfibre strands are first sprinkled into the bits that are hardest to reach before the resin impregnated matting is stippled in with a brush and rollered, to make sure it is fully flush with the inside of the mould. The bodyshell is made up of several sections that are laid-up individually, then bolted together to harden as a single unit.

This capsule may look more like something Jacques Cousteau would have gone exploring the ocean bed in, but it is in fact the mould for a Griffith bodyshell. Bodies are left overnight for the fibreglass to harden, before being united with their chassis and placed five at a time in the curing oven, which takes two to three hours.

The mould for the underside of the Chimaera shell consists of the car's inner wheelarches, floorpans and transmission tunnel, and of course the raw material is laid-in from the underneath. Once that has been done it will be mated with the upper portion. After hardening for eight hours, the mould sections are broken open by air-rams supplied by numerous suspended compressed air lines. In former times the workforce used crowbars to lever them apart to pop the body out.

This Griffith shell – with Chimaera shells beyond – has recently emerged from its mould. The shells are coloured a shade of khaki at first, turning pale creamy yellow as the effect of air and light hardens them still further. The 'flashing' or excess fibreglass material that occurs in places like the windscreen surround, door-shuts and apertures for the rear lights will be pared away during the next phase.

The bodyshells are still too soft to be mated with their chassis, and a lot of preparation has still to be done. In places where the body sections joined together in the mould, small flash-lines will have been created where excess fibreglass penetrated the crack between mould sections, and obviously these, along with air-bubble pin-holes, have to be ground down, sanded off, filled, and flatted off again. This is a very dusty environment, and most operators wear masks and goggles.

Modern TVR moulds have been designed to minimise the amount of flashing that occurs during the laying up process, and these fresh Chimaera shells are remarkably free of extraneous material, even compared with the quantities of excess that came with the later S models. The underneath has to be scrutinised, and there are a lot of apertures to clean the wafer-edges of flashing off, including those for head and tail-lights, indicators, number-plate lights, radiator air intakes, and stereo speakers. Seat belt mounting points are bonded into the bodyshell.

Closures such as doors, boot and bonnet lids are produced separately, and in some cases, the doors for example, there are inner and outer skins. Here, an outer panel receives a bit of a pruning from a hammer and chisel.

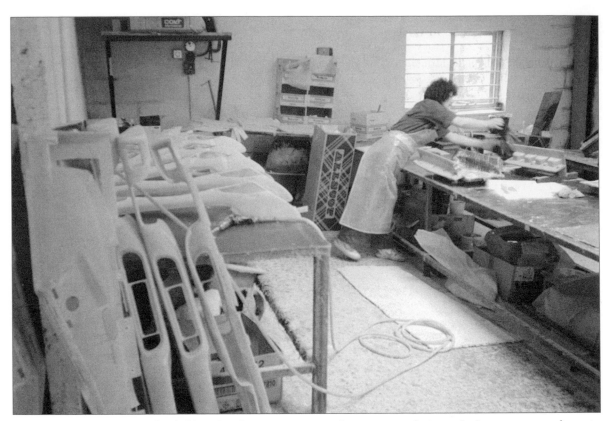

Inner panels that constitute the dashboard and transmission tunnel cover are made in much the same way as the main body sections, only on a smaller and more delicate scale, so they are finished off and prepared using finer compressed-air sanding tools.

This lady is using a roller to impregnate the glass-fibre matting that will go to make up a Chimaera inner door panel. While no less important than making the major components of the bodyshells, these tasks are performed in workshops off the main body shop.

In the inner realms of the body shop, this Griffith now consists of chassis and bodyshell, but there is still a lot of remedial work to be done on the body, including removing flashing in the rear-light aperture and cleaning off the inner rim of the boot space. The body is secured to the chassis by twenty-four mounting points. There are two on the transmission tunnel, two behind the front valance, a pair in the front of each foot-well, four under each seat, another two behind each seat, and four in the boot.

A Griffith 500 body fresh out of the mould, showing the flash lines where the body sections abutted in the mould, and a fair amount of over-matter within the windscreen and around the edge of the engine bay. This one appears to have already found a driver.

A Cerbera in the finishing area, showing where blemishes have been filled in and flattened down, particularly on the lower valance, the roof, engine bay and door-shut. At lower right, its neighbour is upside down while its underneath is attended to.

After the finishing process, each body-chassis unit is wheeled though gigantic rubber curtains into the priming area. The bonnets and doors go through the same process, and are rested on these trestles while sanding with wet-and-dry paper is carried out during the priming process.

These chassis and suspension components are lined up ready to be put through the powder-coating process. Each item is hung up on hooks on a travelling conveyor, and sprayed by one operator with a phosphate that will provide a key. Once an oven's-worth of components has been accumulated, the convoy passes slowly down the narrow corridor of the spraying tunnel. Two men lean in through doors in the side and spray-coat everything with epoxy powder, which clings electrostatically to the metal. The dangling ensemble passes slowly on into the 50ft long oven chamber, where it is cured for 20 minutes at 200 degrees centigrade. Everything is then dispatched to the appropriate point in the assembly process.

Still fully masked, this Cerbera has emerged from the painting booth after being sprayed with two-pack metallic British Racing Green. Customers can opt for any one of ICI's 12,000 colour options, and there are around fifty choices in a range. In the painting booths — one for the bodyshell, another for doors, bonnet and boot, the sprayer naturally wears protective clothing and is fully masked-up with breathing apparatus. He works swiftly, moving the spray-gun from side to side and applying the pigment in short, almost continuous bursts.

A consignment of TVR Power/Rover V8 engines and gearbox units is in the process of being moved into the factory's Assembly area. The engines were sourced direct from Land Rover at Solihull, and rebuilt at TVR Power's factory at Bedworth Road, Longford, Coventry. The process of turning the basic off-roading engine into a high-performance sports car motor was a long and comprehensive one. It began with boring and honing the block, dynamic crank balancing and machining each cylinder head to optimise inlet and exhaust gas flow, and blueprinting the whole unit to exact dimensions and tolerances. The V8 nearest to us has the plenum chamber set up for left-hand drive.

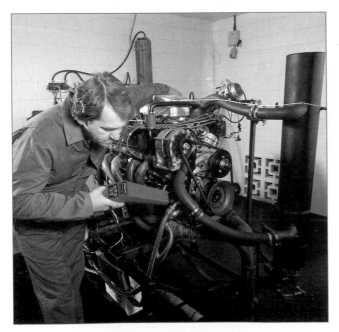

Complete Rover V8 engines are set up and bench tested to obtain optimum power and torque output on TVR Power's pair of Superflow dynamometers. A computerised print-out of the results enables the operator to make further fine-tuning to the set-up. Engine Management systems are made up here, as well as the catalytic converters, while gearboxes are also made to order, and casing for the 4.3-litre transmission is made in house by the AJP department.

Lines of Chimaeras and Griffiths wait to be trimmed and have their engines installed in the main Assembly area, photographed during a routine tea break. They have yet to have their doors fitted, and their flanks are shrouded to protect them from accidental damage during the subsequent operations.

Chimaeras nearing the end of the assembly line in 1993, during a lull in activities, with a TVR Power/Rover V8 dangling from a hoist prior to being inserted into a waiting engine bay.

Using an engine hoist, the TVR Power/Rover V8 lump is lowered very carefully into place in the Griffith's engine bay, while the gearbox is directed below the bulkhead. With no windscreen fitted yet, access is easier for guiding the engine in.

In the trimming department, a section of hide is glued on to an inner door panel. It is a complicated shape to cover, and getting it right calls for a firm hand and careful stretching of the leather. Some six hides are used in the process of upholstering a Chimaera or Griffith.

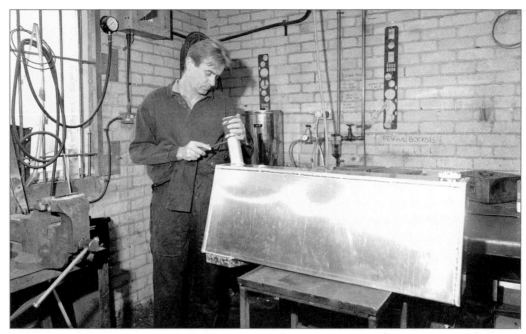

TVR is becoming increasingly self-sufficient – rather at odds with the rest of the specialist motor manufacturing industry, which tends to buy in componentry and simply assemble it. However, the fuel tank is one item that TVR has made by an outside supplier, and before fitting they are tested in the machine shop to make sure the seams do not leak.

Carpeting a Chimaera means gluing previously cut-to-size sections of Wilton on to the sides of the transmission tunnel, floorpans and boot surfaces. The edges may be trimmed in contrasting leather piping. One of these cars consumes 40ft of carpet.

Chimaeras come off the ramps at the end of the old assembly line having just had their propshafts connected up and exhaust systems mated to their gargantuan manifolds and main catalysts.

When the new factory building came on stream in 1995, the larger assembly area provided a much more spacious working environment. Here are some Cerberas nearing completion.

CHAPTER SIX

THE SOUND
AND THE FURY

There's nothing to match the spectacle of twenty or so full-blooded Tuscan racers battling it out round a race circuit. The cacophony of the 4.5-litre V8 engines provides a stirring soundtrack to the thrills of sustained wheel-to-wheel combat as they vie with one another for supremacy at somewhere like Brands or Cadwell Park.

Mark Hales guides the Cerbera AJP8 round Druids hairpin during the National GT Championship round at Brands Hatch on 27 August 1995. Note the sizeable rear wing it's carrying. Opposition in this series consisted of highly modified Porsche 911s, GT2 Lotus and Marcos LM500s.

The Tuscan was originally planned as a 300bhp road car, but based on the success of the racing 420SEAC Peter Wheeler decided a one-make race series would be a good idea for the Tuscan and brought out the Griffith as a road car instead. One-make series have always promoted close and often alarming racing, and at the Motor Show in 1988 TVR introduced the concept of the TVR Challenge, and by February 1989 the prototype was testing successfully. They produced thirty-five cars for dealerships and private individuals to run, plus a couple of cars for the Chairman and a 'guest' driver. The first event was staged in 1989, with thirteen rounds the following year, and it has since gone from strength to strength — to become the world's fastest one-make series. This was a car run for ex-F1 World Champion Nigel Mansell in 1994, when it was the first to try a new lower front air-dam and rear gurney spoiler.

Rear view of the Nigel Mansell Tuscan, showing the additional gurney spoiler. It was also fitted with new 18in x 9in OZ wheels shod with Bridgestones, and lap times promptly came down by 1.25 seconds.

The Tuscan cockpit has a plastic tonneau over the passenger side, so it is effectively a single seater. And being a race car, the dials and switchgear are far more rudimentary than a road car. Warning lights are crudely labelled, as are kill-switches for the ignition and fire extinguisher systems.

Tuscan drivers are protected by a complex roll cage, consisting of hoops and triangulated supports that link up all the way around the perimeter of the cockpit. The trusses are wrapped in foam padding at certain points, in case the driver's helmet strikes them.

The driver can afford to be nonchalant in this case, because the Tuscan is on the rolling road and not full-tilt round a circuit. This is the Clayton rolling road at the TVR Power workshop in Coventry, one of only two such facilities in Europe capable of handling a sustained 500bhp and bursts of up to 600bhp. The car was used to promote TVR Power and driven in the 1991 and '92 seasons by employee Chris Webster.

The works car used by Peter Wheeler in 1993 sits in the paddock beside its transporter. Factory race manager John Reid and the Tuscan department staff built it on a lightweight stainless steel chassis, constructed by Tig welding which took seventy-five hours to assemble, compared with a regular TVR production chassis that would be built in eight hours. It also has a Dynema and carbon fibre body. Weighing just 725kg, it was so light that it had to carry ballast to race at the minimum weight limit of 800kg. On the car door the driver is identified as 'Hopeless', which was certainly not the case.

Not only does racing improve the breed, but there's also something reassuring about a make of car when the owner and Chairman races them himself. A true enthusiast, Peter Wheeler has staunchly played his part for TVR, just as Martin Lilley did with a Griffith in the 1960s, and he has been a consistent mid-field campaigner in the Tuscan Challenge series. Now he gets his speeding 'fix' on the track, he claims to have slowed down on the road.

Peter Wheeler tucks into the apex of Druid's hairpin at Brands Hatch while having his first race in the lightweight carbon-fibre body and stainless steel chassis Tuscan. It will do 0–60mph in 3.7 seconds, and storm up to 100mph in 7.6 seconds, hitting 130mph in 12.7 seconds. Clearly, with so much power available, there's every opportunity to lose a Tuscan, and every corner is a battle with oversteer.

Like all TVRs the Tuscan has a distinctive rear-end. At rest in the Oulton Park pit lane in 1993 is the Mark Hales Tuscan. All racing cars need sponsorship to cover the costs of preparation, entry fees and maintenance. And this car was sponsored by a variety of firms including Eurodata, CarPlan automotive chemicals, Hospital Plan insurance services, and *Fast Lane* magazine. The series itself was sponsored by Mobil 1.

Trying very hard at Snetterton's Esses is Mark Hales in the *Fast Lane*-sponsored car. As well as being a professional motoring journalist, Hales was a former Group A and Porsche 968 driver, and a frequent winner in the Tuscan Challenge. He dominated the championship in 1992 when he was caught on film in this excellent Mary Harvey shot, and was champion in 1993 and '94.

The action is fast and furious as the leaders hammer down to Donington's Redgate corner during a Tuscan Challenge round in 1993. Chris Hodgetts leads from Mark Hales and Colin Blower. All now semi-professional drivers in their mid-40s, Hodgetts was British Touring Car champion for Toyota in 1986 and '87, and went on to race for the Marcos National GT team. Hales emerged as the series Champion in 1993, while Colin Blower was the oldest hand at TVR racing, having competed in the 1970s with a 3000M, and prepared racing cars at his Hinckley garage.

Another close call, and this time Redgate corner is contested by two of the top Tuscan specialists, John Kent and Colin Blower. Kent was driving Giles Cooper's TVR Centre car, while Blower was in charge of the Harrogate Horseless Carriages model.

TVR racers par excellence: John Kent shares a joke with Gerry Marshall in the pits at Donington in 1990. Kent had just beaten Marshall for the victory, which explains why he looks more pleased. Another long-time TVR racer, Marshall made a significant impression on the author with his three-wheeling antics with a Griffith in the 1960s.

Tuscan maestro Steve Cole gets it spectacularly wrong heading out on to the Brands Hatch Grand Prix circuit, applying too much throttle at Surtees bend in 1991, the year he took the Challenge title. The Liverpudlian newsagent and sandwich bar owner is normally at his best on a wet track, although he's noted for an aggressive temperament in a tight situation.

A bit of friendly advice from an old hand: Colin Blower explains where the loos are to Jamie Campbell-Walter as the cars form up in the paddock prior to a Tuscan Challenge round.

It's the calm before the storm, as the Tuscan challenge grid is all set for the off. This is the Thunderbolt Trophy race at Brands Hatch 1996, with the Troy Dunlop car in the foreground. On the right, mechanics prepare their signal boards on the pit wall.

Tuscans are pretty much identical, although there are a few minor variations. Seen here being fired up in the Oulton Park paddock in April 1995, Simon Wayne's Fast Car Clinic team car has slightly different air intakes on the nose.

The Tuscan's 4.5-litre TVR Power/Rover V8 power unit contains pistons and con-rods developed by Cosworth, camshafts and rocker gear from Crane in the States, a custom-made crankshaft, and AP competition clutch, along with special valves and valve springs. The engine is fed by a quartet of Dell'Orto carburettors, and it produces some 400bhp at a screaming 7000rpm. Performance in a car weighing only 820kg is just amazing.

This is a 5.0-litre AJP engine fitted in Jamie Campbell-Walter's Tuscan. The exhaust trunking is as tortuous as that of the Rover unit, and the air filters are clearly different to those of the TVR Power/Rover V8. The filters that are clearly visible on top of the bonnet can identify cars running AJP engines. The AJP unit is 50bhp more powerful than the old Rover-based engine, and by the mid-'90s they were de rigueur in the Tuscan Challenge. This engine produces more torque than any other normally aspirated petrol engine of equivalent size and weight, which helps explain why Tuscans can lap at around the same time as the highly sophisticated BTCC Supertouring saloons.

True to form, here we find Tuscans going every which way at Mallory Park's hairpin in 1996. At the centre of the action in the GK Racing Tuscan AJP8 is erstwhile Morgan hot-shoe Matthew Wurr.

Tuscan racers are all made at the TVR factory, and are built in a similar way to the road-going models. Here, the upper mould for the rear and centre section of the 1998 Tuscan is made ready at the factory's body shop.

In a corner outside the factory paint shop – with freshly painted Cerberas going through in the background – work progresses on the creation of a Tuscan racer. Its bonnet is upside down on the left. Because of the attrition rate in Tuscan racing, the machine shop produces a steady trickle of replacement chassis so competitors who have wrecked their cars can be up and running again as soon as possible.

Peter Wheeler's car will almost inevitably be the state-of-the-art Tuscan, since all new ideas and settings will be tried first on the factory car. Here it is in the paddock at Castle Combe in 1997.

It was predictable that the Cerbera would be developed as a competition car, ultimately with a view to racing at Le Mans. Here is the Andrews/Hales/Loudoun car in the pits garage at Silverstone during practice for the 1996 FIA GT race. Manager of TVR's GT racing programme is John Swinscoe, and the racing Cerbera GT is sponsored by the Harrogate Horseless Carriage Company, and its first win was at Donington in 1997 in a BRDC GT race.

ACKNOWLEDGEMENTS

While compiling this book I was absolutely bowled over by the friendliness and generosity of TVR owners and members of the TVR Car Club, many of whom provided me with an abundance of photographs and information on their own cars, as well as pictures snapped at races and club events. I'm especially grateful to Martin Lilley for his own contribution of archive pictures, as well as his help in monitoring photographs and captions relating to his tenure of the company. He laid to rest several TVR 'old wives tales' that had become enshrined in stone, such as the Tina being named after Gerry Marshall's daughter (it was the other way round, apparently), and the Tasmin being named after a girlfriend. It seems there never was a girlfriend called Tamsin. It wouldn't have been possible to have compiled the book without the help of the TVR Car Club, and the TVR factory, so many thanks to TVR Engineering Ltd, especially Ben Samuelson and Neill Anderson.

In alphabetical order, I should like to thank the following people for their contributions, even if some of their offerings were eliminated at the editorial/design stage because of pressure of numbers:

Jack Acres (400SE and West Sussex area TVR club outings); Chris Alford (himself in action during the 1970s); Paul Askill (Taimar); Mike Bailey (Griffith); Roger Baines (3000S); John Barker (Tuscan racer); Nick Beagley (Tuscan Cobra); Steve Beresford, whose parcel of pictures gave the postman a hernia (Griffith/Tuscan); Keith Bird (Grantura Mk 1 and Microplas Mistral); Ernest Blakeman (Mark III Grantura); Jonathan Bloohn of Phil Stott Performance Engineering (racing Griffith and Tuscan and the restored Mongoose); Ian Blore (350i); Kevin Brazendale (Mark Hales' Tuscan); Simon Bridge (Griffith); Roger Brookes (Taimar); Dick de Bruyn (Grantura 1800S Mark IV); Mr J. Burnham (Tasmin Coupé); Laurie Caddell (Tuscan and Taimar); Richard Carter (1960s archive shots); Vasco Carter (Taimar Turbo); Roger Cook (Grantura); Stan Cook (1600M, the actual *Autocar* road test vehicle); Giles Cooper (fabulous Tuscan racing pictures); James Crofts (enough photos to illustrate a whole book, especially Tuscan racing shots); Guy Dirkin (for allowing me to refer to his in-depth research into the wide-body Tuscan V8s and providing a couple of pictures); Jaki Dors (Dave Farrell's S3); Oliver Edwards (Al Way's Jomar); Jasper Gilder (Haughins supercharged 350 SX and all the background information on it); Bernie Hartnett (Vixen-bodied 2500); Norman Hawkes (Trident coupé); Roger and Chris Johnson (Grantura restoration); Nigel Keeling (Tuscan V6); Julian Knapp (DG Motorsport Griffith); Hubert Leferink (S2, 3000M and 3000S restoration project); Neil Lefley (Tuscan V8s and the Trident convertible); Martin Lilley (for correcting and adding his personal anecdotes to the text, as well as delving into his personal archives for some rare pictures); Stewart McCarte (3000S Turbo SE); Len Messenger (Chimaera); Sarah Millard (Vixen S2); Craig Polly (2500M and the story of its restoration); Mr R. Purdell (Taimar Turbo SE); John Reid, Tuscan race manager at the TVR Factory (for photos and background on Peter Wheeler's Tuscan and his own Vixen racing car).

Steve Reid of Classic TVR (Mark III Grantura and background information); David Rourke (2500 Vixen); Marq J. Ruben (2500, and transatlantic liaison); Gerry Sagerman (for personal anecdotes); Alex Saidel (for historical insights into the Jomar episode); Hans Scheur (Haughins 350i); Jared Silver (transatlantic liaison and artwork of Gerry Sagerman's racer); Steve Smith (Mongoose); Jeff Statham (420 SEAC racer – the actual factory car); Ted Walker (works Mark IIA Grantura race car); Graham Ward (his TVRs and masses of other people's, and early brochures and factory promotional literature); Neil Ward (350i); Chris Weaver (V8S and others); Chris Wright (TVR action shots including his 350i Convertible and Coupé and V8S); Richard Wright (for background on TVR2). The factory's own contribution was kindly provided by PRO Ben Samuelson and his assistant Sally Hunt. The company's chassis and suspension director Neill Anderson helped with specification data. I took most of the factory shots of the cars in production myself while researching a book on the marque back in 1993.

The TVR Car Club's archivist Dave Yeoman helped identify one or two cars, and finally, thanks very much to Carol Folkard at the TVR Car Club (telephone 01952 770635) for helpful liaison and the pictures she supplied. I should also like to commend all at Sutton Publishing, especially Simon Fletcher, Annabel Fearnley and Sarah Fowle, who made this book such an enjoyable project. I'd like to dedicate it to my eldest daughter Kerry who's a TVR fan.